WELCOME
HOME

WELCOME
HOME

INSIDER SECRETS FOR BUYING
OR SELLING YOUR PROPERTY

A CANADIAN GUIDE BY

SARAH DANIELS

WILEY

John Wiley & Sons Canada, Ltd.

Library and Archives Canada Cataloguing in Publication Data

Daniels, Sarah, 1964-
    Welcome home : insider secrets for buying or selling
your property / Sarah Daniels.

ISBN 978-0-470-15973-6

    1. House buying—Canada. 2. House selling—Canada. I. Title.

HD1379.D26 2009   643'.120971   C2009-905191-5

Production Credits
Cover design: Adrian So
Interior text design: Adrian So
Typesetter: Adrian So
Printer: Printcrafters Inc.

John Wiley & Sons Canada, Ltd.
6045 Freemont Blvd.
Mississauga, Ontario
L5R 4J3

Printed in Canada

1 2 3 4 5 PC 14 13 12 11 10

ENVIRONMENTAL BENEFITS STATEMENT
Using 3125 lb of Rolland Enviro100 Print instead of
virgin fibres paper reduces John Wiley & Sons Canada,
Ltd. ecological footprint by:

TREES	SOLID WASTE	WATER	AIR EMISSIONS
27	1,688	15,931	3,707
FULLY GROWN	POUNDS	GALLONS	POUNDS

It's the equivalent of :
Tree(s) : 0.6 american football field(s)
Water : a shower of 3.4 day(s)
Air emissions : emissions of 0.3 car(s) per year

In memory of Pops.

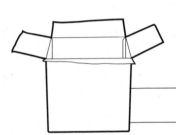

CONTENTS

ACKNOWLEDGEMENTS

There are many people to thank for their help and support in writing this book, and though I would love to mention everyone by name, I may forget a few, so suffice it to say that I would like to thank everyone I have ever met. There, I'm off the hook!

A big thanks to all my pals in the real estate community, in particular, my co-workers at Bay Realty, a truly great place to work. I'd also like to acknowledge the gang at Exclusive Mortgage for answering my many questions. I have to mention my realtor/lunch buddies Ron Robinson and Fern Abercromby by name—if only because it will gall both of them so much, it's worth it.

Special thanks to my book agent, Brian Wood, who first approached me with the idea of writing this book. (It's all his fault.)

Of course, a big shout out to my brother and business partner Philip Du Moulin, who picked up the slack when I was on deadline, among other things.

Finally, thanks to my parents, Patricia Du Moulin and the late Bill Du Moulin. I know Mom is proud, and I know Dad was.

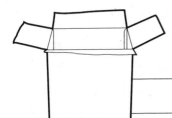

INTRODUCTION

So, you're thinking of moving. Congratulations! Just think: a brand new home, a fresh new start—hey, maybe even some new furniture. It's all very exciting, right?

Well, buying a home should be a lot of fun, and selling a home shouldn't be the main cause of your indigestion and crumbling marriage. Unfortunately, that's not always the case. In fact, when you're dealing with what is most likely the largest asset you will ever own, chances are the stress alone will take its toll. So, imagine how much better things might go if you actually had an understanding of the whole process. Sure, every province and territory follows different procedures as far as real estate is concerned: varying closing costs and commission rates for realtors—you name it. But that doesn't mean you can't go into buying or selling your home (or both) without some helpful tools that can aid you in picking the right realtor, get your financing sorted and get the best deal regardless of whether you're buying or selling.

You don't think you need help? When I bought my first home, I actually bought it privately. The home owners didn't have a realtor to represent them and neither did I. In fact, the owners were family friends. So, you can imagine how that might make for an awkward negotiation. I wasn't a realtor at the time—I was a traffic reporter for a local radio station. Though I had always followed the real estate market, I didn't know the first thing about a real estate contract and the clauses I should include. I didn't order a house inspection, and that cost me at least $1,000, as it turned out the place needed a whole bunch of re-wiring. (And it was just a 900-square-foot cottage. Can you imagine the cost for a larger home?) The wiring was, in fact, a fire hazard, and my first clue was that the cottage went dark when I plugged in a toaster.

Being on a shoestring budget, that $1,000 was a real financial strain. So was the surprise I had at closing: nobody had told me about the closing costs in British Columbia; the Property Transfer Tax here is 1% of the first $200,000 of the purchase price and then 2% of the balance. I found myself paying an extra $2,400 when I signed all the paperwork, simply because I didn't know about the transfer tax.

Unfortunately, ignorance of costs doesn't get you off the hook, and if you haven't budgeted for those expenses, you might find yourself in a great deal of hot water.

So, have I turned you into a nervous wreck yet? Well, don't be—because once you get the hang of some of the basics of real estate, you'll be good to go. You don't need your real estate license—all you need is the information in this book, and your own common sense. ENJOY!

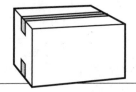

PART 1

GETTING READY

1 MORTGAGE FINANCING 101

If you are buying or selling a home, chances are you're going to need a mortgage broker. If you've already been through the process before, consider this chapter a refresher course. But for first-time home buyers, this step is essential. In most cases, when you purchase a home, a portion of it will have to be financed. (For those paying for a home entirely in cash, please feel free to buy a second copy of this book for a friend. You can afford it!) So, exactly how do you go about getting a mortgage, let alone qualifying for one?

MORTGAGE BROKERS

In the last couple of years, there's been an upswing in the prevalence of mortgage brokers in Canada, and as far as

I'm concerned, that's a good thing. Why? Because a mortgage broker does all the hard work and negotiating for you. They shop you to various financial institutions and will help you find the best financing and terms to suit your needs. That's not to say you can't go to your neighbourhood bank and apply for a mortgage, but it has been my personal experience that you may not get the best rate. That's because banks don't post their best rates in the window, and many people who are looking to buy and are not experienced in the process will not challenge the posted rate, let alone know if there are other financial instruments available that might better suit their needs.

I had exactly such an experience. I owned a home in which I had more than 60% equity, and was planning to sell it in a hot seller's market. I had found the home I wanted to buy, and put in an offer, which the seller accepted. Like many people, I had been with the same financial institution for a long time, so with my accepted offer in hand, along with my income statements and recent tax returns, I trotted off to the bank. I sat down with the banker with whom I had the appointment, and handed her all my information. She sat, saying nothing, as she leafed through all my files. I could feel my cheeks getting warmer. You know that feeling like you're a naughty little kid caught with your fingers in the cookie jar? As I began to explain myself, she looked at me and left the room, leaving me to sit, feeling nauseous, for what seemed like an eternity. Finally, she came back into the office and sat down. Looking across from me, she said that she felt that I would need to make my offer "subject to sale"—or have my father co-sign the mortgage for me! I could feel steam coming out of my ears.

I had a good income, savings and lots of equity in my present home. Was she kidding? No offense to my father, but he was retired at the time, I definitely had a higher yearly income, and I was 41 years old! Grabbing my folders, I stomped out of the bank and pulled out my cell phone. I called a mortgage broker who also happened to be a friend. It was a Friday afternoon at three o'clock, and I envisioned spending the weekend developing an ulcer, not knowing whether I would get financing. After talking to my friend and explaining my position, he told me not to worry—consider it done. In fact, he couldn't believe there was even an issue! It turns out that the branch manager of my bank was pretty surprised, too; he found out what happened from the head of my real estate firm. It turned out that my company did all its banking through that branch. Apparently, the branch manager was not impressed.

So, that might sound like a bitter, cranky realtor hitting her midlife crisis (probably true), but I have a truck load of similar stories. For example, the client who almost signed for a five-year closed rate of 6% when a mortgage broker got her 4.65%; and the clients who went out house hunting thinking they were pre-approved by the bank (they even had the paper documentation), only to have the plug pulled on them. A mortgage broker came to the rescue, once again with a better interest rate.

Banks are becoming more proactive, realizing they are losing business, and have since set up mortgage broker divisions within themselves, using mostly their products. I firmly recommend that if you want to remain at the bank or financial institution you currently work with, that you do not deal directly with the branch; rather, talk to the mortgage broker arm of the institution.

Many prospective buyers try to go it on their own, but what they don't realize is that every time you apply to a different bank for a mortgage, you get "dinged" on your credit rating. That's because every time your credit rating is pulled by a bank or credit union, it's considered a credit application, regardless of whether you end up dealing with them. When you deal with a mortgage broker, your history is pulled just once; the broker uses that one "pull" to market you to prospective lenders.

I have had many clients who have gone to their bank and been offered a rate that has ultimately been bested by a mortgage broker. What amazes me is how many people will go back to their bank and ask them to match the better rate: when the bank does, they sign with them on the dotted line. My question is this: if they weren't willing to do the best they could for you initially, why would you let them have your business?

Ultimately, a mortgage broker does all the heavy lifting for you. Once you have filled out a mortgage application and they have pulled your credit rating and history, they can also help you improve your overall rating by advising you on credit card use and the like. The best part is that all this costs you absolutely nothing. A mortgage broker is paid by the lending institutions. They are literally competing for your business, even in an uncertain credit market.

WHY DO I HAVE TO GET FINANCING STRAIGHTENED OUT NOW?

The reason you're doing all this now is so you don't have to be disappointed, frustrated and possibly even fuming later. If you're kicking around the idea of selling your home and buying another, you need to know exactly where you stand. For instance, you may be self-employed, and on your income tax return your stated income may actually be less than what you earn, since you're running income through your own company. You might think you can qualify for a larger mortgage, but the paperwork says otherwise. Similarly, you might be under the impression that you won't be able to qualify for much in the way of financing, when it turns out that because of low interest rates or having 20% or more down, you might be able to spend a little bit more on a home than you thought—and it might actually cost you less. Confused? Your mortgage broker will explain it all, and tell you the maximum dollar amount you can consider paying for a house, and what your weekly, bi-weekly or monthly payments would look like. This will give you a feeling of confidence when you go out house hunting, and will prevent you from falling in love with a property you actually can't afford, or settling for one home when you could have had another.

So, how do you find a good mortgage broker? Realtors often work closely with several of these professionals, and they will happily provide you with referrals. Realtors are a good resource when looking for a mortgage broker, as they obviously have a vested interest in their clients getting the best rates and terms: a happy buyer is a *good* buyer! But you don't have to rely on realtors alone: friends, relatives and work colleagues who may have recently bought a home are also a good source of such information. Many mortgage brokers, much like realtors, have their own websites, and will be happy to supply a list of satisfied customers. Like any client, you want to be treated promptly and efficiently, so if you call a mortgage broker and don't hear back from them in 24 hours, move on. When you do find a mortgage broker who fits the bill and with whom you feel comfortable working, find out what financial institutions he or she deals with and why. Ask the broker to give you different scenarios for your financing needs, and see what he or she comes up with.

INTEREST RATES, AMORTIZATION
AND ALL THAT JAZZ

We've been pretty lucky over the last several decades; interest rates declined steadily throughout the 1990s, and have, for the most part, stayed at historic lows through much of this decade. The rise or fall of interest rates is vitally important, however, because even a one-point change can have a substantial impact on the mortgage amount for which you will qualify.

The interest rate will primarily be defined by your credit rating and the amount of money you have as a down payment (the more money down, the more equity you will have in your home—and often the more desirable you will be to lenders). A traditional mortgage in Canada requires a 20% down payment; if you were to purchase a home for $500,000, you would then require a down payment of $100,000—which would not include closing costs such as property tax and any other title transfer taxes that may be levied in your province. Both your mortgage broker and your realtor will be able to advise you of those costs, so make sure you keep them factored into your financial equation!

Any other property purchase that includes a down payment of less than 20% requires mortgage insurance. The amount is calculated on a percentage of the total mortgage, and does not boost the actual interest rate charged on the mortgage itself. Currently, there are two major mortgage insurers in Canada: Genworth and the Canada Mortgage and Housing Corporation (CMHC). AIG still does insure Canadian mortgages, but they are now more on the fringes of mortgage insurers.

Here's an example. You've got a $50,000 down payment, and your mortgage broker has approved you to carry a mortgage up to $500,000. That gives you a total of $550,000 to spend. We'll assume that you have a very good credit score, so the mortgage insurance rate you will be paying is the lowest available, 1.5%. We'll imagine that you actually purchase a home for that magic amount of $500,000, which means that minus the down payment, your mortgage will be for the amount of $450,000. That is the amount that needs to be insured. So, you would be charged a one-time fee of 1.5% on that $450,000, which could be added to your mortgage and amortized into your payment. This is what it would look like:

$50,000 = down payment
$450,000 = mortgage
1.5% = interest rate charged on mortgage amount (one-time charge) to insure it
So: $450,000 x 1.5% = $6,750.

The insurance on your mortgage would add $6,750 to the cost of the home. Like I said, you are not obligated to pay this in a lump sum; that cost can be added to the mortgage amount and factored into your mortgage payments.

Of course, that 1.5% rate is reserved for the best quali-fied clients—the rate can jump as high as 5% and beyond in some cases—often considerably higher than all other closing costs combined. Again, this is a great reason to be in touch with a mortgage broker as soon as you even consider purchasing a home. With their know-how and advice, you'll have an opportunity to improve your credit rating and ultimately reduce your costs and qualify for a better interest rate.

For a brief time in Canada, you could secure a mort-gage with an amortization of up to 40 years—meaning that the cost of the amount you were borrowing would be spread over 40 years. Now, the maximum amortiza-tion is 35 years, with the average mortgage amortization falling between 15 and 25 years. When you take out a mortgage, you will agree to either a rate of interest to be paid over a set amount of time, meaning your payment will remain the same during that term, or a variable rate, in which case your payment may fluctuate depending on the interest rates. A lower interest rate means you will pay down your principal faster; higher interest means the opposite. In recent years, variable rates have been

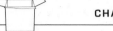
very popular, with Canada's interest rates sitting at historic lows.

USING THE MONEY IN YOUR RRSP
TO BUY A HOME

The Home Buyers' Plan (HBP) allows you to withdraw up to $25,000 (or $50,000 as a couple) from RRSPs to buy or build a qualifying home for yourself (as a first-time home buyer) or for a related person with a disability. It is important to thoroughly check that you meet the necessary qualifications. You may still be considered a first-time home buyer if you own a rental property or if you have not recently owned a home.

This is a temporary "loan" from your RRSP—you must pay back the amount you borrow within 15 years or it will be added to your taxable income. There are many exceptions to all of this: for the most part, you can use this program only once—a one-shot deal, so to speak. There are a variety of rules to be followed and qualifications to be met, but outside of that fact, you have to look at the possible negatives.

Yes, you will save, in a sense, by borrowing from yourself. But at what cost? The money that could be earned tax-free while in your RRSP will in most cases outstrip the cost of borrowing, which is why many investment counsellors will advise their clients to borrow money to put in RRSP accounts. If you have taken losses in your RRSP account, cashing out would only permanently lock in those losses, and not give stocks or mutual funds any time to recover. The cost of borrowing is, in most cases, less than the earning potential the RRSP account would have otherwise. However, if you have no other funds to use for a down payment, this might be the way to go. The best solution here is to have a long discussion with a financial advisor, and another with your mortgage broker. They will be able to crunch the numbers to help decide whether using your RRSP is a wise idea.

INTERIM (BRIDGE) FINANCING

Interim financing, also known as bridge financing, is temporary financing required to complete the purchase of a new home, if the home you currently own has either not sold or has a firm offer but has not yet reached its closing date.

If you will be using the money from the sale of your existing home as a down payment on a new property but don't yet have this money, then you will need interim financing to bridge the gap. Let's say you bought a new home that you absolutely love—and knew that you'd lose the opportunity to purchase it if you waited to sell your current home. So, now you technically own two properties—something that's going to be costly. If you have sold your first property by the time you have to complete the purchase of the new home, but the closing date (the date you get paid) isn't until a month after you have to pay for the new one, you'll need interim financing. This type of financing can be expensive, so it's always best to have the sale of your existing home and possession of your new home coincide. Remember, as well: you *might* qualify for financing if you haven't got a *firm* offer on your current home by the time you're expected to close on your new home, but you also may not. Make sure that when you speak to your mortgage broker you ask what would happen if you ended up in this latter situation. Most lenders would classify this as buying a second property, and you would have to have enough equity in your current property, as well as qualify income-wise, to carry both homes. Lenders would generally not view this as interim financing, but instead as conventional financing. Any changes in the real estate market, particularly one that is trending downward, can significantly impact you in this case, as would any increase in interest rates.

Some lenders offer interim financing directly, while others will leave it to you to find the funding elsewhere. It is important to know—before you get into this situation—that interim financing can be reasonable, but it some situations it can be very expensive!

The bottom line is that no matter what: always discuss every possible scenario with your mortgage broker.

When your offer on a property you wish to purchase is accepted, make sure you fax a copy to your mortgage broker, and make sure that everything passes muster. The lender will most likely require an appraisal of the property to ensure the value matches what you've offered. If you are purchasing a strata property, in some cases the lender will want to see some of the financials. Always ask questions! Remember, your broker is there to help you purchase, not to put the kibosh on your new home. Work with your broker—and he or she will work for you.

2 DOING YOUR "HOMEWORK"

So, you've gone to the mortgage broker and a lender has outlined what you can afford and what your monthly payments would roughly be. The next step is to figure out where you want to live.

URBAN VS SUBURBAN

Ah, the age-old dilemma—to live in the city or head to the suburbs, or maybe even farther afield. Depending on your age, this decision can be easy or very difficult. It can often be a question of the head wrestling with the heart.

Most of us, when we are in our 20s, would never consider living in the 'burbs. A house, two kids and a minivan? The horrors! Truthfully though, most twentysomethings wouldn't want to live in the suburbs, anyhow. If you're in your 20s and in a position to buy, first of all, I commend you. Secondly, if you're anything like I was when I was 26 and bought (with the help of my parents) my very first condo, you couldn't afford to live in the suburbs, either. For most young first-time buyers, especially singles, the lure of the city is overpowering. With convenient public transportation links, nightlife and employment opportunities, it just makes sense that if you're in your 20s and single, Wisteria Lane is *not* calling. (And FYI, the residents of said lane don't look like they do on TV, either).

So the location debate tends to start for young couples, especially those who are planning to start a family, be it in the near future or, say, five years out. Though we've all heard (and I always drone on about) the importance of location, sometimes location and budget do not align smoothly. We'll touch on other aspects of this age-old push-and-pull later in the book, but suffice it to say, depending on which city you live in or near, and in which province, your dollars will only go so far. For instance, in Vancouver, a recent check showed fewer than 50 detached houses in the entire city limits listed at less than $500,000. However, in the nearby city of Surrey, a Vancouver suburb, a similar search revealed more than 700 listings. So, as much as you may want to live close to the heart of the action, if you want the dream of a house and garden, your ideal location may have to take back seat.

However, many young families are now sacrificing space for the convenience of city living. Major cities such as Toronto, Vancouver, Calgary and Edmonton, to name just a few, have seen their condo markets expand and in some cases explode as people decide to pass on the suburbs in favor of a deluxe apartment in the sky. With their workplace within walking distance, and cultural attractions and influences all around, it has become the new dream of another generation. After all, people have raised families in apartments in such major cities as London, New York and Hong Kong for years, so why not here? In general, this type of living means a sacrifice in personal space. However, with many families having only one child and the green movement becoming more prevalent, for many the idea of a 3,500-square-foot home with a two-car garage seems like a thing of the past.

Remember, too, that if you're buying with a partner, both of you should be sitting down with this book in hand (!) and figuring, out exactly what you want. It's as simple as making a list. If your spouse or partner has always dreamed of a fast-moving city lifestyle, but *you* can hardly wait to get an address on a cul-de-sac, now's the time to make sure that you make a decision that will incorporate both of your wants and needs, along with some compromise. If you don't manage that, you won't need this book anymore—you'll need a book on how to save your relationship.

So, here are some more things you should have on your list. This will also help you narrow your location, as what you consider non-negotiable will help you figure out where you actually will end up focusing your search, based on your budget.

RIGHT-SIZING

If you and your significant other have been brought up in traditional 2,000-plus-square-foot homes, there's a good chance you may want to stick to what you know. Both parties need to figure out what kind of space you can live with. For instance, if you have to have a home office and you want a playroom for the kids, then you've automatically added at least 400 square feet to your criteria. If you're someone who would be considered a packrat or your closets runneth over with clothes and shoes or sports equipment, you might need a basement, garage and a home with a great deal of storage space. To determine which case applies to you, take a good long look at the place you live in now. What about it do you love, and what's driving you nuts? I'll be honest, one of the reasons I sold my last home, though I loved it for a lot of reasons, was because it didn't have enough closet space. Truth be told, I have too many pairs of shoes and boots, as well as a bit of a handbag obsession, and the home certainly would have had enough storage space for most people. But it ended up not fitting some of my criteria, and so when I stumbled upon a home that met more of my needs, it was time to move.

Others may be looking to downsize. Many older couples, when left with an empty nest, decide to find something smaller which often is also less expensive to maintain. It's probably also proactive, because who knows when those kids are going to try and come home and live rent-free in the basement! In reality, the upkeep on a home that is really only half-used can be a big unnecessary expense. Heating costs alone can make monthly bills skyrocket. Of course, downsizing can occur in all shapes and sizes. I had an older single woman come through a 3,500-square-foot home on a large lot, all remodelled and ready to move in. She said she was downsizing, but even this house was *too small*. However, she was downsizing from more than 7,500 square feet, so I guess everything is relative. You get the point, though. Focus on what you can live with, take into account how that will affect your budget and ultimately your location.

GET ON THE 'NET

You've calculated your budget and you know what you need space-wise, so now it's time to figure out exactly *where* you can consider purchasing your next home. If you have decided you want to live outside the city because it suits your budget and square-footage requirements, then figure out which areas are going to have the kind of homes that suit you. Websites such as **MLS.ca** are very handy, as you can log in your basic requirements and it will spit out a host of properties that may fit the bill. Not only that, the site's mapping ability allows you to pinpoint areas of interest. If you have school-aged children, you may be more interested in homes a short walking distance to school. You'll also be able to get an idea on how far your commute might be, as well as sort out transportation links if you use public transport.

Never rule out any area, since you just never know what you'll find. For instance, I live in the city of White Rock, BC, about a 35-minute drive south of Vancouver. I had never even considered moving out of the city until I decided to move up the property ladder. I could barely afford a larger apartment in the city, yet on an afternoon drive, I discovered I could own a (small) home in a great neighbourhood for less! I didn't know anyone in White Rock, but soon found there were lots of people my age in the neighbourhood, I was close to great restaurants as well as the beach, and all the shopping I needed was only four blocks away. What's not to like? Thirteen years later, I'm still here. Which brings me to. . . .

GET IN THE CAR

After you've done your Internet surfing, it's time to get in the car and drive. Much like my road trip to White Rock, you need to actually go to those targeted neighbourhoods and drive around. What do you see? Obviously, you want to find something like neat, orderly homes or condos, clean streets, accessible shopping—all the things that make it a place you would want to call home. Does the area appear safe? If you're looking for a family environment, are basketball hoops a common sight over garage doors, or bikes on the front lawn?

Consider making this trek on a Saturday or Sunday, the days you would typically find open houses. These opportunities enable you to meet local realtors and confirm what you can purchase within your price range. ASK THE RIGHT QUESTIONS: find out how long the property has been on the market, how long the owner has been there, why they are moving, etc. Remember—don't judge a book by its cover: check out everything, even the homes you know are not the right budget or size. This will help you get a feel for the pricing in the area. Most people are shocked to find out what homes in their own immediate neighbourhood are selling for, so if you're willing to go a bit farther afield, this type of hands-on research can bring great results.

Remember, don't make knee-jerk decisions. I can't tell you how many clients I've had who were moving from other locations and wanted to look only at homes in certain neighbourhoods based solely on what friends *who didn't even live there* had told them! I honor the request for short while, but always take them to other parts of town that I know they'll like. Four times out of five, they end up purchasing a home in one of the areas they saw with me, not the ones recommended by their friends. If you're serious in finding a home that you will be happy in for the long term, you cannot wear blinders.

* * *

The next chapter is devoted to finding a realtor. Your realtor should be based in the area you want to buy in. Your realtor's familiarity with the pros and cons of different neighbourhoods, and knowledge of current market conditions, are the key to making the buying process more efficient and (hopefully) fun.

Though I work primarily in the area where I live, like many realtors, I also sell in other areas I know well. When I do, it's usually as a buyer's agent. To find a realtor to represent you as a buyer, consider the following: obviously, you'll meet realtors at open houses—this is a great time to ask questions about their knowledge of the neighbourhood. Ask for business cards, but don't feel pressured to give your personal information. If you feel you're being put under the gun, such a realtor may not be the right one for you.

Don't sign anything you don't feel comfortable with, such as a Buyers Agency Agreement. This is much like a listing contract; in short it, obligates you to work with the realtor with whom you signed the agreement. Though realtors are told it is in their best interests to have clients sign these agreements, I never do. Who wants to force a client to work with them? If a buyer wants to work with me, I am happy to work and work hard. Chances are you feel the same way: if you feel comfortable working with someone, you'll be loyal to them, and vice versa.

The important thing to remember when you start looking at homes with the realtor of your choice is to have an open mind. Be clear with your realtor about what you're looking for and what your price range is. Most realtors have access to programs that will put you on an auto-notification system; this means when new listings come up, they can be emailed to you at the same time realtors get them! But keep your parameters wide: you might be surprised at what you may like, as opposed to what you thought you'd want. If you trust your realtor, you may end up with something just perfect that you never would have even considered previously. Yes, you might have to look at a lot of new listings before you find the "one"—but if you narrow your search too much, you might miss a great opportunity!

3 HOW TO FIND A REALTOR WHO IS RIGHT FOR YOU

So, this is it! You're ready to head out the door and start shopping for your new home—or conversely, invite realtors into your home to help you sell it. This should be the easiest step you take, right? Wrong. While most realtors have access to the same tools, real estate websites, and avenues for advertising, it's the way that your realtor employs those resources on your behalf that counts. In addition, you and your realtor have to work from a place of trust and the goal of a happy outcome. It's crucial that your personality and that of your realtor's are well matched. If you like to keep things strictly business, you may be more comfortable with a realtor who presents themselves in a suit and tie and keeps any discussion outside the realm of real estate to a minimum. However, if you're a "jeans and T-shirt" kind of person, you may be more comfortable with a realtor whose personality is a little more laid back. It works both ways: on the few occasions I have attempted to work with clients whom I did not "enjoy" as people, I have always regretted it.

"I'VE SEEN HER SIGNS EVERYWHERE ..."

It's not a big surprise that when people begin to think about buying or selling a house they start noticing realtors' signs prominently displayed on the front lawns of properties listed for sale. A multitude of "for sale" and "sold" signs creates an impression that a certain realtor is doing a lot of business. However, that doesn't mean that particular realtor is right for you.

If you're selling a property, one of the first things you should do when creating your list of potential realtors is to look at those who specialize in the type of listing you have and in the area in which you live. Why would you work with someone who seems to specialize in high-rise condos when you're looking to sell a pre-war bungalow? When you're buying or selling in a competitive market, you need to be working with someone who has expertise in the area of your focus.

Back to all those signs: are they all saying "for sale"? Or are there a lot of "sold" stickers on them? Obviously, the latter is the clue you are looking for—but remember, properties lingering on the market may not be the fault of the realtor. It won't hurt to ask why those homes aren't selling. Is it price? The property itself? The location? Realtors will often end up in the position of having to list a property at the vendor's (inflated) price. If so, it may take time to encourage the vendor to reduce his or her price to a more reasonable level and hopefully encourage offers.

A good strategy when looking for a realtor, is to take the time to attend open houses in your neighbourhood or in areas you're looking to buy, and talk to the selling agents. You don't have to disclose any personal information, so don't feel pressured to do so, but you can definitely get a feel for how the realtor works. Remember to keep an open mind, as realtors who may not seem as "busy" can be just as efficient at helping you buy or sell a property.

CHECK THE LOCAL ADVERTISING

As I mentioned, all realtors have access to the same type of tools—it's just a matter of how efficiently and effectively realtors use them. In a competitive market, advertising can be key, and that's because not everyone who buys a home— or sells one for that matter—simply decides one day that they want to move. I, myself, am a perfect example: I was quite content with my previous home until I tagged along with my brother and sister-in-law to check out an advertised open house for a property they were interested in buying. It turned out that the house didn't have enough room for my brother's family, but it was just right for me (and my dogs). I moved; my brother and his wife did not. It's a textbook case of a realtor advertising a home and attracting a buyer who wasn't even thinking about relocating!

The Internet and **MLS.ca** and similar sites are great places to start your search for a realtor. In this computer age, I believe it's a necessity that realtors have their own website, particularly if they're working in a competitive environment in urban areas. But even rural realtors, who deal in acreages, farms and vacation properties, will find that websites first and foremost will help buyers and sellers connect. A great way to see who is advertising what on the Internet is to Google (or Yahoo or whatever search engine you prefer) the realtor's name and see what pops up.

Once you've found some websites, start comparing the amount and quality of information. There are many tech companies that provide website formats to realtors, and some are designed to provide information more clearly and attractively than others. How easy is it for you to access the different areas of the site? Are there any special features, such as uploaded floor plans or virtual (photo) tours? How well maintained is the site? For example, are the listings up to date? If you've driven by a realtor's sign for three days but can't find that particular listing on his or her website, that might indicate a problem. In this world of instant gratification, people want information right away. If they can't find that listing, they may skip to another realtor's listings. That will be particularly annoying if drive-by viewers are skipping *your* listing, if you're the seller.

In addition to researching the Internet, also read through listings in the real estate section of your local newspaper. Realtors advertise properties by neighbourhood—an expense that generally comes directly out of the realtor's pocket. See what catches your eye. It doesn't necessarily have to be the realtor with the most listings; look for photographs that highlight a house's curb appeal—clever write-ups and well-designed ad spaces. If a good ad is catching your eye, it's doing the same for others, too. There are lots of people over a certain age (and you may be one of them) who are not comfortable on a computer, and print ads may be where some buyers go first to find a new home.

The way a realtor advertises a property can give you an idea as to how they would work for you. A creative ad could indicate a realtor who thinks outside the box when helping you search for your dream home. (It could also mean they have an assistant who is an advertising genius, but let's not get paranoid here!)

TALK TO YOUR FRIENDS AND NEIGHBOURS

So, you've checked websites, looked at neighbourhoods that interest you, perused the local real estate papers and narrowed your list of realtors to three. Now, put that list aside and talk to people you know and trust and who live in the neighbourhood that's on your location list. In particular, talk to people who have moved within the last several years. Sure, you may have a friend who swears by the realtor he used 10 years ago, but you really need to judge a realtor on their current performance. This part of the process is where things may get interesting—and contradictory. That superstar realtor you might have been thinking was at the top of the list might not be such a strong performer in their former clients' eyes. Another agent you didn't really have on your radar may be the type who goes beyond the call of duty—and clients appreciated it. ALWAYS ASK FOR SPECIFICS. If people you talk to express unhappiness with their realtor, ask for the reasons. If the answer is something like, "I told the realtor not to disclose that the house has a major foundation issue that would likely not get picked up in an inspection (also known as a latent defect), but he disclosed it anyhow and it cost me money …", well, I think I would side with the realtor because the realtor is legally (not to mention ethically) bound to disclose such an issue. I'd also question my friendship with the owner of said home.

The feedback you're looking for from the people you talk to is whether their (realistic) expectations were met. Did the realtor return calls in a timely fashion? Was he or she able to give helpful advice in regard to the purchase or sale of the home? Did he or she seem to have a sincere interest in the clients' well-being? Were they happy with the realtor's pricing strategy, and did they feel it was effective? Did they appreciate the realtor's marketing efforts, or did they feel they were lost in the shuffle? A common complaint clients have about realtors is that once the listing contract is signed, they never have another conversation with their realtor. Remember, your realtor works for YOU. That's why you're paying them a commission—and that makes you the boss.

RESEARCH COMMISSION RATES

When you sell your house, you pay a commission. There is no standard commission rate across Canada; in fact, every province seems to have its own status quo. For instance, in British Columbia, full-service realtor commission rates are commonly 7% on the first $100,000 of the value of the listing, and 2.5% of the balance. This rate is divided between the realtor representing the buyer and the realtor representing the seller. So, if a property sold for $500,000, the commission would be $17,000 (plus GST). Yes, that's right—GST rears its (ugly) head everywhere. Since the realtor provides a service, this service is subject to GST. If the province you live in has HST (harmonized sales tax: currently in effect in Newfoundland and Labrador, Nova

Scotia, Quebec and New Brunswick proposed to come into effect as of this writing in B.C. and Ontario July 1, 2010) you will pay both GST and PST, as the two taxes will be blended into one.

In provinces such as Ontario, the realtor may work on a flat commission rate: anywhere between 4% and 6%, again split between the buyer's and seller's agent. That will put the commission rate for a full-service realtor on a $500,000 home between $20,000 and $30,000, plus GST or HST. Again, these are not standard rates and all commissions are negotiable. Remember, too, that other taxes may apply to the sale of your home that have nothing to do with the actual commission. Make sure you understand what your closing costs will be in advance, to avoid surprises. Your realtor will be able to help you with this, and I'll go into more detail later.

When asked about commissions, most realtors will carefully explain where the money goes: to pay for advertising, office fees, car expenses and, of course, their time. Remember, typically, the realtor does not make a dime until the sale of the house closes. If a home does not sell, or the seller decides to take it off the market, the realtor does not get paid for the time and effort he or she has expended on the listing. In a very active market, especially one that's vendor driven, you may be able to negotiate commissions with realtors. Do not expect the same in a buyer's market, as it will often take longer to sell a home, thus driving up the time spent and the marketing costs that a realtor will incur.

It's pretty easy to find out what the standard commission rates in your area are by calling local real estate offices.

INTERVIEWING YOUR CANDIDATES

At this point, you should have a short list of candidates. It's time to start making some phone calls.

A good indication of how your relationship with the realtor you choose will proceed is how quickly your initial call is returned. But again, appearances can be deceiving: I've been in situations with clients where I have been unable to return calls for several hours. If that's the case, chances are the realtor will make that clear.

Tell the realtors why you've contacted them. Let's say you have a condo to sell: a two-bedroom, one-bath home, 925 square feet, in a 25-year-old low-rise building. Give them the basic information and ask if they could come over and provide an evaluation. Remember that you've done some homework here; as discussed in the previous chapter, you know what has sold in the neighbourhood and hopefully you've got your "realistic" goggles on.

Try to schedule the realtors' visits on a day or evening when you aren't rushed. Expect to spend at least an hour with each realtor, so make sure you allow ample time. The realtor will most likely tour your condo, take notes and try to figure *you* out.

Is the realtor telling you what you want to hear?

Let's face it—we all think we have great taste and have decorated our home in a way that would make Martha Stewart green with envy. But while you might feel your kitchen sets the standard for perfection, potential buyers might think it's dated and small. In fact, we've probably all gone to a friend's home and gushed over their new master bedroom furniture, even though you personally might think it looks like it belongs on the set of an adult movie. You'd never tell them that, though!

It's a realtor's job to tell you these things. Well, they might not be *that* honest, but they should be able to delicately nudge you in the direction that you need to be heading (and we'll get into that a bit later).

Here's a great example of what you *don't* want to hear: "Oh, my, what stunning taste you have! What a beautiful home! Did you purposely not match the kitchen appliances? How original! Is there a reason the powder room has no finished flooring? Oh—you couldn't decide ... yes I'm sure the buyer would be happy to finish that room, etc., etc."

You get the picture. The realtor you choose should remark on the best features of the home, while pointing out issues you might have overlooked. For example, you might be a fan of bold colours, but in most cases a home painted in neutral tones, accented by colour in the furniture or art, will be more attractive to buyers. The majority of buyers don't relish seeing a home decorated head to toe with wallpaper, as they think ahead to having to scrape it off the walls or painting over it. Never assume that what you think is a minor makeover is not going to be a significant turnoff to a potential buyer. Another red flag, even though it may be easy to fix: carpeting in the bathroom. It enjoyed a brief period of popularity, (though I can't imagine why), but it's widely considered unhygienic since it provides a breeding ground for mould and bacteria. If you have it, get rid of it.

Don't be swayed by the realtor who comes to you with a listing price that is significantly higher than other valuations you've been given. This is a trick of the trade called "buying a listing." Simply put, a realtor might come in with a bunch of comparables that indicate your home should be priced much higher than you expected. Heck, I'd be thrilled too—who wouldn't want to have an extra 10% to put in the bank? *But make sure you get a full explanation as to how they arrived at that number.* Look carefully at those comparables: are the houses in the same neighbourhood? Are they close in terms of square footage, lot size, upgrades, age and curb appeal? Most importantly, make sure the homes the realtor is using as comparables are of similar style. You can't compare a three-bedroom ranch bungalow—a "rancher"—with a four-bedroom, two-storey home. I don't care what anyone tells you. You want the most exact comparisons possible. If you choose to ignore the facts now, it will come back to haunt you later.

Here's a story that illustrates this point:

Recently, one of the realtors in my office told us during our weekly meeting about a new listing he just signed up. The address seemed familiar: it had been listed previously (with another broker and agency) for a substantially higher price than my colleague was listing it for. The seller had been a long-standing client of my colleague, but decided to shop around this time, as he was sure his home was worth more than what my colleague valued it at. Six months later, the seller was back to list with his original realtor, and he brought along the presentation the previous realtor used to convince him he could obtain a higher price. What an interesting presentation it was! Not only were the comparables often in better overall condition, with more upgrades and in neighbourhoods with higher values, but they were often completely different styles of homes, with larger lot sizes! The presentation was pretty flashy, full of self-congratulatory stories about the realtor and masses of statistics that seemed to bolster the rationale for the high valuation. It all looked very professional, yet the comparables used had little bearing on setting the proper listing price and fair-market value of the home.

To make a long story short, my colleague listed the property with a new price and marketing strategy (after it had languished on the market for six months with the other realtor). It sold within a month. The lesson here? Don't fall for flash. Do your homework, and when someone brings you a presentation, don't be fooled by flattery.

WHO WILL HANDLE SHOWINGS?

For those who may have pets, or may not be comfortable having strangers in their home, knowing how showings will be held will be extremely important. Many realtors use lockboxes, which are basically key holders accessed only by other realtors who are showing the home. This would generally mean that the realtor you've hired is not present for viewings. This might not be an issue if the property is vacant, but if you have an indoor-only pet, such as a cat, or a dog who is an escape artist, you may want your realtor to be present for all showings. Or, you may have an alarm system, and are comfortable giving the code to YOUR agent, but not everyone else's. In this case, you should make sure that the realtor that you hire will be able to attend all showings. In other cases, you may be required to let other agents into your home. If you aren't comfortable with this, say so. I generally avoid having my sellers have any direct contact with buyers, as it can personalize a relationship that should remain business only. Keep this in mind when interviewing realtors!

ASK THE RIGHT QUESTIONS

At the end of the realtors' presentations, it's time to ask questions. Make sure you have a pen and paper handy when you meet so you can take notes. Here are some examples of what to ask the realtor:

- How did you arrive at the price you're suggesting we list for?
- How are you going to market the property? Can we see your plan and comment on it?
- How much exposure will our house receive on your website?
- Will you be advertising in the local real estate papers?
- How many open houses are reasonable to expect?
- Will you be present for showings or will you let prospective buyers and their realtors into our home?
- What advice do you have for us in terms of upgrades that are reasonable for us to do?

You should be comfortable asking anything: remember, the realtor will be your EMPLOYEE!

One important but touchy issue you could face could be cancelling or terminating the listing. Ask prospective realtors whether they will release you from the listing contract unconditionally if things aren't working out. Be prepared, especially in a soft market, for a realtor to agree, but conditionally: you may have to reimburse his or her costs if you're planning to re-list with someone else. Cancelled listings are different from terminated listings; to terminate a listing means neither party is under any further obligation, whereas a cancelled listing will often mean that you cannot immediately list with another realtor, and if you were to sell your home within a certain time frame, even privately, you may have to pay a commission to the realtor you "cancelled" with.

Probably the best advice is to go with your gut. You'll always work better with someone who suits your style the best. If you're more laid back, you may want to work with someone with a similar personality. (Of course, "laid back" should not be code for "lazy.") You want someone whose marketing style works for you, and whose advice and guidance you trust.

THE LISTING CONTRACT AND PROPERTY DISCLOSURE STATEMENT

Congratulations! You've chosen a realtor, and you're happy with the decision. Between the two of you, you've hammered out an asking price you are comfortable with. Now, it's time to sign the listing contract. This is the agreement between you and the listing realtor that sets all the terms and conditions that both parties must abide by. Every province uses different listing contracts, but for the most part they contain the same information. You should always review *any* listing agreement with your realtor so you're aware of exactly what you're signing. If you feel pressured at all, DO NOT SIGN. Visit my website for samples of listing agreements used in various provinces, and the terms and conditions that you most likely will find. I haven't found one that stated you had to give up your first-born child—yet!

At the beginning of the contract, you'll find the basics. Your name will appear as the owner or "seller." Anyone who is on title must be shown on the listing contract, and that person or their estate or power of attorney must sign the contract for it to be valid. If, indeed, it is an estate or someone holding power of attorney that is signing the contract, documents supporting their authority to sign on the seller's behalf must be submitted as well.

The listing contract is actually made between you as the owner of the property and the listing brokerage. Your realtor is your representative from that brokerage. The seller gives the brokerage (in most cases) the right to list the property in question for a certain time frame specified in the contract, starting at a set date and effective until 11:59 p.m. on the expiry date, unless it is renewed in writing.

By signing the contract, you will be allowing the listing agent to gather and otherwise obtain any information concerning the property from any persons, government bodies or corporations, and to share this information with other parties. This means your realtor can collect copies of surveys, septic system information, occupancy permits, building permits and anything else that may be on record for the property.

You will also be agreeing on terms and details: how much commission will be paid to the realtor, and what portion of that will be used to pay any realtor representing the buyer; what will happen if the listing realtor represents both buyer and seller (dual agency); and what duties the listing realtor will undertake as part of the contract.

The property disclosure statement (PDS) is generally filled out at the same time the listing contract is completed. Again, the questions the PDS pose vary between provinces, but it's really a snapshot of the property from the perspective of the owner. The most important thing about the PDS is that, when incorporated into the purchase contract, it can be used against the owner if it can be proven the owner withheld or provided misleading information regarding their knowledge of the subject property. NEVER omit ANY pertinent information the PDS calls for. To do so could cost you a sale, or a lot worse. You'll see what I mean later in the book.

There are several other forms you might run into along the way when either listing your home, or beginning the search with a realtor. Every real estate board has different requirements: some realtors will ask you to sign forms regarding the payment of commission, others will not. Remember, you are signing a contract, so make sure you review it thoroughly and ask questions. Be sure to visit my website to see these forms.

Questions to Ask Your Realtor

1. What types of properties do you primarily sell?
2. What do you do to market the property?
3. Do you advertise, and where? How familiar are you with the area?
4. Do you have a website? If not, why? How will you market my property?
5. Are you willing to hold open houses?
6. If you were to list my home, what list price would you suggest and why?
7. What would you suggest I do to improve the sale-ability of my home?
8. Are you present for showings? (Important for pet owners in particular.) Do you use lock boxes?
9. What is the commission rate?
10. Will you terminate the listing if I am unhappy?
11. How long have you been in the business—and what's your track record?
12. Can I expect regular feedback from showings?
13. Can you provide references?

4 | THE PROS AND CONS OF SELLING YOUR OWN HOME

It's human nature to want to retain as much of your investment in your home as possible. Home owners who are considering putting their house on the market are likely to ask themselves, "Really, how difficult can selling my own home be?" Alternatively, maybe there's money to be saved in using an agent to sell your home, but not a full-service realtor so you won't be paying full-service commission rates. There is absolutely nothing wrong with trying these routes, and there are many success stories. But you need to make sure that going it alone, or with some help, is the right avenue for you. There are many pitfalls you need to be aware of if you decide to go it alone.

Obviously, most people will take this direction with the idea of saving money. In a seller's market, this strategy can work for you. With properties in demand and inventory that's not staying on the market long, you may have success with a "for sale by owner" listing. Word-of-mouth on a good property may help overcome the lack of Internet exposure on such popular realtor-driven websites such as **www.mls.ca**. Properties listed with a discount broker (a realtor who offers the very basics in sales support, often with no marketing or advertising aside from **mls.ca** for a lesser commission) will also see interest. It works because, generally speaking, in this type of market, buyers and their agents have to work fast. Hot markets are often the result of a low property inventory and a surplus of buyers, so the reduced commission may be overlooked by the realtor. You may wonder why the commission should even be an issue, and I will touch on that soon.

A buyer's market is a completely different story. When you have a surplus of inventory and fewer buyers—or even a balanced market with average property inventory and therefore buyers don't have that sense of urgency to purchase quickly—you might find that selling your own home or using a discount realtor can cost you time and may even cost you much more money.

Here's why: to sell your property, you need exposure to other realtors, and the ugly truth is that realtors expect to be paid. As I mentioned earlier, in a seller's market, that reduced commission might not be an issue, and if you are an FSBO (for sale by owner), a realtor may bring you a buyer and make provisions in the contract of purchase and sale for you to pay that realtor a commission for his or her efforts. A buyer's or balanced market means your property is probably up against a lot of competition, and there's not as many people looking to purchase. Realtors may spend months on end looking for properties on behalf of their buyers, and remember, they don't get paid for all that tire kicking. Imagine this scenario: there are four homes of a similar type and price in an area of interest to the buyer. Three of the listings would pay a standard buyer's agent commission and one a greatly discounted rate. The buyer's realtor is taking that purchaser out to look at homes and arranges a tour of potential properties. Unless the buyer specifically asks to view the property with discounted commission, don't be surprised if that particular listing doesn't make the cut. Even if it does, expect the buyer's realtor to write in the full standard commission, payable by the seller. So, with that out of the way, let's look more closely at the topic at hand.

FOR SALE BY OWNER

Be forewarned: if you plan to go the FSBO or discount realtor route, you're going to literally be taking on a second job. Why? You won't have the access to a realtor's knowledge of the local market, the selling prices in the neighbourhood and actual property assessments. Nor will you have the ability to tap into the working relationships and networks that realtors form with each other—this includes knowledge of the local inventory, pricing trends and market perceptions. (Note: some discount realtors provide access to **www.mls.ca** and other agent-supported websites and not much else; others provide some very basic services. Ask for specifics so you know exactly what to expect. For the purposes of this discussion, we'll operate on the premise that you're getting only Internet exposure.)

Also, and this is a big *also*, you will not have the benefit of a professional opinion as to how to maximize your home's potential. Your nosy neighbor who gives you advice based on all the open houses she has attended, and your friend who's sure he knows all about the market based on a three-minute lead story on the evening news, are *not* experts in the field. It may sound like I'm being flippant, but it seems to me that when it comes to real estate, often everyone thinks they're an expert. (I'm sure watching every episode of *E.R.* would not qualify one to be a surgeon.) If you're intent on selling your home on your own, you will need to do a lot of research in order to set a price, properly stage and present your home, advertise and understand the current market cycle.

Ask yourself if you really want to tackle the job of organizing signage for your home (FSBO in particular), advertising (many discount agents don't provide print advertising and FSBOs will not have access to realtor-operated and -distributed local papers); organizing pictures to go online if, in fact, you have access to a website to post your listing; and the real biggie, the day-to-day business of actually selling your home.

Are you going to hold open houses? Open houses get people in the door, but do you know what to do when people start asking questions and express an interest in your property? Have you created a sell sheet with basic information about the square footage, age of the roof and furnace, amount of insulation in the attic, a list of window coverings, appliances and light fixtures that will be sold with the property? What about showings? Will you be in charge of escorting people through the home? Have you thought through how to determine if interested buyers have qualified for a mortgage? Even though I'm a realtor, I would not try to sell my own home. It's just too personal. When I have listed my own homes (I've moved a couple of times), I list the property with my brother, who is also my business partner. Realtors call him, they make appointments through him, they give him the feedback and he negotiates on my behalf. He will tell me what he thinks I should list my home at, and advises me what updates or repairs I should do before I sell my home. He also boots me out for all showings. Why? Because, generally speaking, owners who show their own home say too much, and buyers viewing a property when the owner is present don't feel comfortable chatting amongst themselves, especially if the owner insists on giving a guided tour. The seller who shows his or her own home will often point out what he perceives to be the worst features of the house, or rave about one particular aspect that he or she loves. This can be a real turn-off to prospective buyers, as most people viewing a home want to develop their own thought and opinions, and don't want an overly personal opinion from the current owner.

If you're selling your own home, you will often have to deal directly with the buyer, and you may not know whether that buyer has qualified for adequate financing. Remember my mantra from Chapter 1: the first thing you should do, regardless of whether you're buying or selling, is to get pre-approved for financing by your bank or mortgage broker. A good realtor will make sure their clients have their financing sorted before they take them out house hunting. However, there is no guarantee that the buyer you would be dealing with directly has taken this step. In fact, there is no guarantee that this person is even serious about buying at all: they may just be nosy, or worse. Remember, when you're showing your own home, you also have to take into account that you are inviting in total strangers. You may not know their true motives, and they may not be good. My intention is not to frighten you, but if your house was not up for sale, chances are you would not be inclined to let strangers roam through your home. Sometimes our common sense goes out the window when the prospect of selling our home is the carrot dangling in front of us.

The real problem with going the FSBO or discount realtor route (again, assuming you have purchased only Internet exposure) is that you have to contend with the actual process of selling your home. One of the most difficult issues will be price: will you ask too much because you don't have the market knowledge and you're too attached to the property? Or worse, will you unwittingly sell for too little, just to save commission costs?

* * *

Here's a true story—but the names have been changed to protect the short-changed.

Recently, old family friends, we'll call them the Browns, decided to sell their property. Because it was a seller's market, they figured, "Why pay a realtor commission when we can do this ourselves?" The plan was to sell their home and then purchase in a community closer to their children, and enjoy their retirement. So, instead of talking to local realtors, they asked the bank to give them

an appraisal of their property. Now if you ask most realtors to give you their honest opinion, they will tell you that
bank appraisals, much like property assessments, are not a
reliable barometer of selling prices. They can be wildly inflated or considerably less than what the true selling price
should be. Unfortunately, the latter was the case here.
Armed with their bank appraisal, and a homemade "For
Sale" sign posted firmly out front, the Browns were happy
to accept a full price offer on their property. Even better,
(I say, facetiously) as far as they were concerned, the buyer
would not close on the property for six months in a market
that was on the rise. This meant that the Browns would
not be paid for that property for six months. It also meant
that if they found a house they wanted to purchase in the
meantime, and the seller of that property wanted to close
before the Browns' house closed, the Browns would have
to arrange for interim financing. Though I tried to advise
the Browns against FSBO, I was told they knew what they
were doing. (Thank you very much.)

The truth is, they didn't. The Browns did indeed find
a property that they wanted to purchase (using a realtor
in their desired area this time). And, again, since it was
a seller's market, they had to meet the closing dates the
seller requested. (The property received multiple offers
and sold for more than the asking price.) That meant that
the Browns had to arrange for interim financing. And it

wasn't hard for me to do bit of research and find that they had very likely sold their home for a price considerably less than what a professional realtor would have achieved. I believe that they realize this now, but I doubt that they'd ever acknowledge that. Who wants to admit that they literally left tens of thousands of dollars, maybe more, on the table? The good news is that they saved about $15,000 in commission. At least, I think that's supposed to be good news.

There's more to consider, too. Have you thought about the legal expertise you need? Who will prepare the contract of purchase and sale? How will you handle offers with *subjects*: that is, what if the offer to purchase is subject to a home inspection, or even subject to the sale of the buyer's own home? What amount is reasonable to accept as a deposit and who will hold that deposit? Will it be nonrefundable? There's a lot to consider when you embark on the FSBO route. Discount brokerages will often provide help with these issues, but the amount of assistance and expertise you get depends on what kind of service you have signed up for.

Selling your home really is a full-time job—from making sure the home is well presented and setting the price, to handling the marketing, showings and negotiations, and taking care of all legal aspects. This is all the more difficult when you are dealing with what is most likely your biggest asset and most emotional investment—your home.

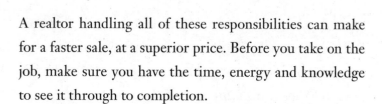

A realtor handling all of these responsibilities can make for a faster sale, at a superior price. Before you take on the job, make sure you have the time, energy and knowledge to see it through to completion.

PART 2

SELL BEFORE YOU BUY

5 GETTING YOUR HOME READY TO SELL

Unfortunately, getting your home ready to sell doesn't mean just slapping a sign up front. If only it were that easy! If you're planning to list your home, and there are issues with the property that need to be addressed, make sure you budget your time and your cash accordingly. The traditional "best-selling" season is spring, and time is of the essence, so you may want to get started on your plans well in advance to avoid any snafus.

First of all (and with the help of your realtor, who will offer advice and make suggestions), you need to be honest with yourself about the actual appearance of your home. Is your kitchen dated? Do walls need a fresh coat of paint? How does the exterior of your property look—have you kept up with the maintenance of your home? Every house is different, and every owner has his or her own budget, but here are some tips that should help you along the way.

YOUR HOME'S EXTERIOR—CURB APPEAL

The outside of your home is its most important selling feature. You might not even notice that the shutters need painting or half the cedar hedge is dying, but trust me, potential buyers will, and the outside appearance of your home may stop them dead in their tracks. Worst yet, they may just drive right on by.

Walk the perimeter of your home: how does the exterior look? If your home has vinyl or aluminum siding, make sure it's clean (but beware of power washers; you could do more harm than good) and check for peeling paint or trim. Make sure shutters are secured, windows are clean and steps to the front and back doors are in good nick (shape), as well as all decks and patios are swept. These areas can become slippery after rainfall, and cracks and other damage can occur if you've had a particularly cold winter. Children's toys, garden hoses and any other items lying around should be stored away. Make sure garbage cans don't get left out for days after pick-up. Don't leave bicycles in the driveway or junk mail on the front steps. It's attention to these types of details that will immediately show a prospective buyer that you care about your home.

Take a good hard look at the roof: do you know how

old it is? If it's at the end of its lifespan, you might want to bite the bullet and replace it; otherwise, you most likely will have to address it when you and your agent set the asking price for your home or when it's time to negotiate an offer. A new roof is an expensive item and you should discuss the pros and cons of replacement with your agent. You might own an older home in an area where properties like yours are being torn down and replaced with brand new ones. In a case like this, spending money on a new roof might not reap any benefits.

And please, I beg of you, if it's not Christmas time, take down the Christmas lights! Hedges should be trimmed, fences in good repair and gardens cleaned and weeded. Remember the garage too: if it's turned into one big junk storage area, now is the time to clean it out. Even better: add some inexpensive shelving. A garage that can't hold a car makes buyers think there isn't enough storage in the house, so now is the time to break any packrat tendencies. This doesn't have to be a budget breaker: most of these tasks can be handled by you and your family.

In addition to the roof, there are some other big-ticket items visible from the outside of your home. Does your home have its original single-pane windows, or have they been upgraded? Windows are expensive to replace, but a buyer will look for energy-efficient windows. Again, the type of home and where you live will help influence the decisions you make here. Obviously, if you have a heritage home with stained-glass windows, you wouldn't replace them and destroy the character of the home. However, simply replacing any windows with seals that have broken (double paned), or broken or cracked windows, shows you care for your home. Lack of maintenance in a home is a red flag for buyers: if you don't care about the things they can see, what about the things they can't?

If your home's exterior is not its best selling feature, use some imagination to create visual interest outside. The following suggestions can be followed according to the season, and even in a snowy winter, the placement of some large evergreens and seasonal décor can make the front of your home stand out.

If you aren't big on gardening, and you want to keep it simple, consider hanging baskets and flower boxes. There are many varieties of flowers that bloom early in the season and are able to withstand colder temperatures. When everything is gray, a pop of colour will definitely draw buyers' eyes to your home. Even hanging a flag, whether it's the Maple Leaf or something else, will give visual impact.

In winter, if you live in an area that receives a lot of snow, ensure that you keep the sidewalk and your walkways shovelled, as well as your driveway if you have one. Again, this shows pride of ownership. In some neighbourhoods, as mentioned, homes may be replaced by new builds

—but many buyers will look at purchasing and renting out the home, and building in the future. Again, this points to making sure your home shows as nicely as possible. It doesn't have to be a designer showroom, but it *does* need to be clean and tidy, as that will reflect the desirability. Yes, it can be a hassle, but it will pay off for you in the future.

I will repeat this mantra throughout. Put yourself in someone else's shoes: what would you think if *you* were looking to buy a home? What about the appearance of the outside of your property would make you want to see inside? We often forget what our own environment looks like—but when you're selling, this needs to be foremost on your mind.

STEPPING INSIDE

Ah, so much to see—but will it make a buyer happy? First of all, let's cover the general stuff that applies to every room in your home—and the number-one rule is: CLEAN, CLEAN, CLEAN. There is absolutely no excuse for showing a dirty home if you intend to sell. No excuse! Not even children, pets or busy schedules. I cannot tell you how many times I have taken buyers out to look at a home, the appointment having been made well in advance, only to arrive and find the property in question to be a complete mess. From dishes left in the sink and dirty laundry on the floor, to (I'm not kidding) unflushed toilets—it's amazing the state in which some people will show their homes.

A clean home cannot be more important—the problem is that many of us have different ideas of what constitutes clean. The answer is: spotless. I'll use a personal story as an example.

I have purchased and sold two homes within the last five years. On both occasions, before I even put the property on the market, I hired professional cleaners to come in and scrub the place from top to bottom. This means cleaning inside ovens and behind the refrigerator, all kitchen cabinets (including grimy fingerprints), all closets, storage spaces, under beds and behind the sofa, under area rugs, all windows, walls, doors and doorknobs, baseboards and crown mouldings. Absolutely everything! As the owner of five dogs, every time I had someone coming to see my home, I would spend at least an hour re-cleaning the place, vacuuming, dusting and anything else that needed to be done. Like anyone with pets, I made sure that I had an ample supply of air fresheners that specifically addressed pet odors. Just because I no longer noticed the smell of "dog that recently swam in the local pond," doesn't mean anyone else wouldn't. Then I would load said pets into the SUV, and out we would go; all dog beds removed and all signs of pets gone.

If you have children or pets, or both, I realize that this will create a bit of a challenge, but you are going to have to make it work. On showing days, make arrangements with a friend to take the family dog for the afternoon, and keep kids out of the house. Cats shouldn't be a problem, but make sure that you let people know that there is a cat in the home (if it is an indoor pet, you don't want people viewing the home to accidently let it out). Birds and any small animals, like the family hamster, can remain as well, but out of the way—keep those cages poop free! Children's rooms are not off the radar either—they must be kept clean. If you have to resort to bribery, I suggest you do it. (I'm sure this goes against everything the pros say about child rearing, but I'm no expert on kids—you might need another book for that.)

You might think that I'm being too strict on this point, that people will understand the stuff that is "everyday living." Trust me: people will not "see past the mess." They will leave. It's a question of making the extra effort. If a buyer sees five houses in one day, and four of them are not up to snuff, your odds of receiving an offer may be better. Pride in your home goes far.

Of course, every room has its specific needs in order to get it in that "ready for sale" condition. We'll start with the most important room in the home.

The Kitchen

First of all, take a cold, calculating eye to the kitchen. What are the things that you would most like to change about it? Chances are, it's the same thing buyers will notice. This doesn't mean you have to remodel, but it does mean you might need to spend a few dollars. If your cabinetry is looking a bit tired, and it can easily be painted a neutral color, you might want to start there. New hardware on cupboards always helps. Wallpaper borders should be removed: they were popular in the '80s but they are *not* popular now. If the room itself is in need of paint, find the time to do it. For a small room, white might be the best option. If the flooring is shabby, there are lots of tile and vinyl options: again, this is all relative to the price point your home falls into, and you should discuss this with your realtor. For instance, if you have a starter home in an area of starter homes, don't splash out on $15,000 worth of granite countertops. The investment might not be worth it.

However, using the same example, it might be worth your while to install new appliances if your present ones are more than 10 years old. First-time buyers are attracted to homes where they don't see a lot of additional expenses. Obviously, new appliances aren't in everyone's budget, but simple things can go a long way. Keep countertops clear. That means putting the toaster and the coffee maker away, clearing away letters or bills or to-do lists that you habitually leave lying around. The idea is to show a large useable and functional space, so those with small kitchens need to weed out anything unnecessary. This means cleaning out all cutlery drawers and rearranging food storage to show an efficient layout. Buyers are nosy, and they will look at everything. Remove pictures and other decorations off the front of the refrigerator, since they tend to make it look messy. Put fresh flowers on the kitchen table, if you have one, or on the window sill. No dishes in the sink, no breakfast crumbs on the floor. By now I should remind you of your mother: keep that in mind every time you question whether something really needs to be done!

The Bathrooms

Again, the condition of, and upgrades to a bathroom can really be a deal breaker. Let's not kid ourselves: in our everyday lives, the typical bathroom has leftover toothpaste in the sink, towels haphazardly slung over towel racks and waste baskets full of Kleenex and dental floss. Unfortunately, buyers are not interested in your grooming habits. This room will also benefit from brutal scrutiny, and proper storage and a sparkling clean appearance will be your best friend. Ideally, the room should be a neutral color, with no aging or peeling wallpaper dating its appearance. Hopefully your bathroom toilet, sink and bathtub or shower all match, but if you have an avocado green toilet, you might want to budget for an upgrade.

Proper lighting is always an easy way to make your bathroom look a bit more upscale, so if the fixtures are dated, consider investing in an inexpensive but more modern look. Flooring should be clean and in good shape. Make sure grouting is up to snuff and scrubbed. If you have a shower curtain that has seen better days, replace it. A clear shower curtain is inexpensive, and can give the appearance of a larger room. Keep the toilet bowl clean and the lid down. MAKE SURE THE TOILET HAS BEEN FLUSHED, I BEG OF YOU.

IF YOU HAVE CARPETING IN YOUR BATHROOM, REMOVE IT ASAP, NO IFS, ANDS OR BUTS. Carpeting is extremely unhygienic and will put off ALL buyers. Clean bathroom counters, and put all makeup and other grooming items such as hair dryers, shavers and curling irons out of sight. Anything left out should be displayed in a pleasing manner—a pretty Kleenex box, a matching toothbrush holder and soap dispenser. Remove the 17 different shampoos and conditioner bottles from the shower or bath—it just looks messy. And a discreet air freshener certainly won't hurt. Keep towels folded and hung up properly, put those that are not in use away. This is particularly important if you have just one bathroom, as it must show as clean, airy and large enough for all that live in your home. I personally always suggest a set of white towels in the bathroom, as they look fresh and modern, and they look good with any color scheme.

The Bedrooms

Again, it's all about editing. Remember, you don't know if the buyer of your home will have young children, teens or no children at all. The idea is to appeal to as many people as possible by presenting a pretty but relatively neutral canvas that they can see themselves moving their furniture—and their lives—into. If your eight-year-old convinced you to paint her room bright pink with a purple border, it's time to tell her that the room will now be painted a taupe or pale yellow—something that doesn't define the room in the buyer's mind as "eight-year-old child's room." Remember, the fact is that you want to sell your home. In reality, what does it matter if the room is no longer pink? So check all bedrooms, remove all posters off the walls, put toys and clothes in hampers or toy chests, and don't allow dishes in the bedrooms—all the usual stuff you try to enforce when you aren't planning to move! Carpets should all be cleaned; if a carpet is seriously damaged or stained, consider replacing it. Every home is unique, and different price points require different solutions.

The master bedroom is no exception. If you can splash out on some new bedding if yours is looking a bit ragged, then do it. Clean the bedside tables, throw out old magazines, clean the chest of drawers. DO NOT FORGET THE CLOSETS! Especially for women, closet space can be imperative. If you have a walk-in closet, start editing out things you no longer wear and pack them up and donate them to charity. After all, why move it to another house? The more spacious your closet appears, the better. If it looks like you're moving because you need more room (which very well may be the case), why announce that to the buyer? Try to make the room look as spacious as possible—this is a great time to ask your friend who watches all those interior design shows to come over and help. Regardless, less is more. That means less clutter, shoes on the floor, no overflowing laundry hampers—you get the picture.

For all other rooms in the home, such as living, dining, family rooms and dens, a good cleaning and de-clutter is top on your list. The dog bed is fine to stay in the family room when the home is not being shown, but get it out of the house if buyers are coming to visit. Fluff up the throw cushions, clean the coffee tables, dust, clean blinds and take a sharp, objective eye to your surroundings. If the curtains are dreary and you can't stand them, get rid of them. Inexpensive sheers can be found at all sorts of stores and will instantly freshen a room's appearance. It may sound like an exaggeration, but if you spend $1,000 or \$2,000 on a few things that will enhance the appearance of your property's interior, you could add many more thousands to your final sale price.

Before you embark on anything, though, do consult with your realtor. As mentioned, some properties may benefit more from some upgrades more than others, and you should be judicious. For instance, if you live in a neighbourhood of high-end homes that have all been tastefully updated, including kitchen remodels in the \$50,000 to \$75,000 range, spending \$20,000 on a kitchen makeover would be a bad move—you'd be better off not to do anything at all and reflect the lack of upgrades in your price. If you can't do it properly to the scale that is expected in the neighbourhood, there's no point in taking on the task. Conversely, don't splash out on all sorts of extras if you live in a starter condo. Nobody is going to spend 25% more for the same condo just because you put in specialty hardwood flooring at \$25 a square foot.

You should also be clear with your realtor as to what stays and what goes in your home. In the market I work in, typically appliances come with the property, and are included in the description. However, that's not always true. (Personally, I think it's best to leave them behind; arguing over a fridge is just not worth losing a deal over.) More importantly, items attached or affixed are generally included in the purchase. That means wall-to-wall carpeting stays, but area rugs go. Built-in shelving stays since it is attached to the wall, but a book shelf unit that is free standing will go.

What can often be a bone of contention are items such as light fixtures—in particular, chandeliers. If you have a family ornament such as this that is attached to the property, it is usually presumed to be included, so you must make sure that those items that fall under such parameters are excluded from both the listing and purchase contracts. To avoid the conflict altogether, you may want to remove the item and replace it with something that fits the bill but doesn't break the bank. You really don't want to be fighting with the buyer over your grandmother's wall sconces on closing day.

While you may be grumbling under your breath and complaining that buyers surely can see through paint colors and a messy bedroom, I'm here to tell you that they don't and won't. If they do, chances are they will low-ball an offer at you. Why? A messy home hardly attracts offers.

This is also the time to de-personalize your property. Put away the majority of family pictures and knick knacks. Remember: small doses. This doesn't mean making your home sterile, but if every table and wall is covered in family photos, it'll be hard for buyers to imagine themselves in the home. It doesn't stop there: you may love your collection of china figurines, but all 150 of them displayed throughout the living room is overkill. And unless you are selling a cottage or something similar, a display of hunting rifles on the wall (or mounted animal heads) can deter prospective purchasers. The same thing applies to religious symbols: there is no way to put this nicely; it's a personal choice and I have had many buyers made uncomfortable by an abundance of religious items.

The best way to get a crash course on what you should be doing to get your home in order is to spend a Sunday afternoon attending open houses in your area. Which homes show the best and why? While you're at it, dropping by new developments is always helpful for ideas, as the show homes are professionally staged and decorated in the latest colors. I am certainly not suggesting you need to have your home professionally staged: this can be very expensive, and is usually cost-effective only in the top end of the price scale. But you may benefit from a stager coming by and taking your own furniture and arranging it in a fashion that best highlights your home, as opposed to actually renting furniture.

Remember: when it comes time to purchase a home, you'll be able to benefit from the sellers who haven't read this book. You'll know to look at the bones of the home, and overlook the bad presentation, having made sure your home showed at its best. Their homes could be languishing on the market longer than the average, all because they didn't prepare—and you might be able to take advantage of that with a lower offer.

Getting your home ready to sell is not always easy, but if you do it properly you'll be able to stand head and shoulders above the competition. Be brutal: most of the things you will be throwing out, giving away or replacing are items you don't need anyway. It won't be easy; so allow at least a weekend to address those things that need tending to. Depending on the length of your list, you may need more or less time. But it will be worth it!

Check List for Getting Your Home Ready to Sell

1. Curb appeal: Does your house have it? Clean up the outside!
2. Remove everything that you don't need: LOSE THE CLUTTER! Store the stuff, and toss the junk!
3. Paint where needed—and keep it neutral.
4. Do the little fix-its, (i.e., patch cracks, replace or repair anything broken, loose, or damaged).
5. Clean floors and carpets, drapes and blinds. Wash down baseboards, walls, anything that collects dirt and fingerprints.
6. Get rid of odours! No smoking in the house, and keep air fresheners handy to get rid of pet smells.
7. Lock away jewellery and anything else of value.
8. If it feels like a hotel, it's ready to sell!

6 PRICING YOUR HOME

Putting a price tag on your property is probably one of the most difficult decisions to make, because it involves market conditions, neighbourhood variables (proximity to amenities, condition of houses), the square footage of your house and comparables (how much have homes in your area been selling for). There is a host of other variables and intangibles. Just because the four-bedroom home down the street sold at a certain price, doesn't mean that your four-bedroom house will fetch the same; it could be substantially more or considerably less. Knowing the inventory of houses for sale and having the pulse of the market will help you determine an optimum price. Even if you have a price in mind, always listen closely to your realtor.

Presuming you have hired a realtor to help you sell your property, the first thing he or she will do is pull up the market comparables. This will include recent sales in your area, active listings, expired and terminated listings and how long said listings remained on the market. He or she will show you which properties saw a price reduction (or, sometimes, a price hike), and will most likely be able to give you more detailed information about market conditions that is not readily available to the public.

NEIGHBOURHOOD

Where you are is often a key consideration. A four-bedroom home in a subdivision 25 kilometres from the city will be priced entirely differently than the exact same home in a residential area close to downtown. You just cannot compare the two. You really can evaluate the worth of your home only by comparing it to those in your immediate neighbourhood. Within that same area, you must note the specific location. Are you across from a park or school? Some buyers may love that—others may not like the idea of having a noisy playground nearby. Is the home located on a cul de sac or quiet tree-lined street? Home owners tend to gravitate to locations like this, as opposed to houses on a busier road, no matter how beautiful they may be. That can provide a price advantage to a home with a better location within the neighbourhood, that may not be as updated inside.

However, every neighbourhood is different. At a trendy downtown address, having a pub and an all-night coffee shop on the next block as your townhome may be ideal. In a more residential family area, that pub and coffee shop may be considered a nuisance to potential buyers and could have a negative impact on the sale of your home.

STYLE OF HOME

Once you have narrowed down the area you will use for comparison, the type of home you have becomes a key consideration. Whether it's a condo, townhouse, semi-detached or detached home, every type of property has subsets within these categories. That means that you cannot compare a three-bedroom semi-detached home to a three-bedroom detached home, even if they are identical in square footage, and the neighbourhood and upgrades are comparable. A 1,000-square-foot, two-bedroom condo will be priced differently than one that is exactly the same square footage, in the same building, on the same floor, but which has a different floor plan that includes a den. Will the two-bedroom condo with bigger rooms be more expensive, or will it be the condo that also has a den? The price difference may be subtle, but it needs to be noted, because in a balanced or buyer's market, in particular, overpricing your home could result in you chasing the market down if values shift.

You'll also need to know the types of homes that are in your immediate comparable area. If you live in a neighbourhood filled with ranch-style bungalows, but you happen to own a two-storey home (that includes a basement), you might have a problem. Those ranchers could indicate that the area is popular with retirees, and your home might not be what that type of buyer is looking for. Meanwhile, those families who would appreciate your home might not be drawn to it, *because* of all those retirees. Who would their kids play with?

Some styles of home sell better than others, whether it is a conventional two-storey home in one area, or a spacious rancher on a large lot in another. But, generally speaking, a two-storey home with four bedrooms will sell better than a three-level split home, even if the square footage and amount of bedrooms are the same. Four-bedroom properties in family areas are often more desirable than three-bedroom units. The penthouse apartment will be worth more than the exact same unit on the second floor. There are always exceptions to the rule, but don't bank on the thought that your property is that exception!

SQUARE FOOTAGE

Even a couple of hundred square feet difference between the sizes of homes can mean a big difference in price. If your home is 1,800 square feet, don't try to price it using comparable homes that are 2,500 square feet. Simply put, they are *not* comparable. Stick to a range of within 10% on either side. For example, if your home is 2,500 square feet in total, use homes that are between 2,250 and 2,750 square feet that meet your other criteria as comparison.

UPDATES

A very important part of pricing your home will be in the updates. You may love your 25-year-old kitchen, and enjoy defrosting the refrigerator once a month, but chances are the modern buyer will not. So, if your kitchen and bathrooms are dated and your flooring has seen better days, your price will need to reflect that. Even after the tweaking you may have done and the hard work you've put in to get your home ready for market, you must be realistic. What you may see as quirks may be seen by potential buyers as flaws or stumbling blocks, depending on how your home is priced. On the flip side, as mentioned in Chapter 5, if you have gone overboard for your area, such as overspending in upgrades for the bathrooms and kitchen that exceed the standard expected for the neighbourhood, you may not be rewarded in your sale price.

For instance, the last home I owned and sold, I added a second bathroom by redesigning some closet and wall space. When it came to the kitchen, I replaced appliances and countertops, but did a relatively inexpensive countertop as opposed to granite, since the expense would not be recouped in the sale price. The size and age of the home, plus the comparable properties in the neighbourhood, made granite countertops an unnecessary expense. If you've completed upgrades beyond the expected standard of where you live, be reasonable when it comes to setting your listing price.

BIG-TICKET ITEMS

The condition of certain big-ticket items in your home can drastically affect the price you will command. If your home has a roof that is one wind and rainstorm away from a leak, that needs to be reflected in your asking price. The same theory applies to wiring, heating and plumbing, not to mention the exterior cladding of your property. If the stucco is crumbling, the chimney bricks are loose and the mortar is deteriorating or the siding is cracked, you will not be able to compete in price with similar homes that do not have these issues. If the neighbourhood average for a roof replacement is $12,000, be prepared to show that in your asking price. Also, make sure to be up-front with prospective buyers. An inspection will show what you may be trying to hide or ignore: a buyer is more flexible when they know the true costs that need to be incurred when they write an offer. A nasty surprise on an inspection report can kill a deal.

MARKET CONDITIONS

In recent years, the real estate market in Canada has seen some spectacular highs, as well as some very real corrections. If you have not been following the real estate market closely, you may not be aware of recent developments. The price you may have been able to get for your property just one year ago may not be realistic today. On the other hand, if you live in an area with strong fundamentals, you may be pleasantly surprised. Do not rely on anecdotal evidence! Your next-door neighbour, the doctor, is not qualified to help you price your home for current market conditions. People tell me all the time about what their "real estate investor friend" told them, or that they should be getting a certain amount of dollars per square foot of home. They rely on this unsolicited advice and information as if it was gospel. It was probably given with the best of intentions, but it isn't accurate.

An example: I had a lovely couple, who were planning to retire, list their home with me. It was at a time when the market was beginning a rather rapid correction, and as I told them, they needed to be aggressive in their pricing. Their home was more than 30 years old, with very few updates but in a desirable area. Within a month, we received an offer which my clients accepted, but the buyers pulled out of the deal. They said they would still like to pursue the home, but as first-time home owners the price they had agreed to was pushing their budget too much. They asked if my vendors would consider reducing the previously agreed upon sale price by $10,000. I begged my clients to accept the revised offer, but they refused, as they felt they needed a certain amount of money to purchase their retirement home. I pointed out that what they hoped to purchase was dropping in price as well, so all things being equal they weren't "losing." They stuck to their guns, something I know they now regret. The buyers moved on to another property, and a housing market that was already on a downturn began to drop substantially. Buyers disappeared altogether, and my clients missed their chance. Five months after they passed on the offer, they would have been lucky to get another bid for $75,000 less than the original. It just goes to show, *you need to know the market.*

On the flip side to this, when a market starts to heat up, you need to act fast. Here's a story that will make your head spin! In February 2009, the real estate market was in the tank virtually everywhere. Between the actual statistics on the economy, and round-the-clock news banging the drum to the tune "The Sky Is Falling," prices on homes were down significantly and buyers were few and far between. At this time, a half-duplex was listed in Vancouver's trendy Kits/Point Grey neighbourhood. It had been completely remodelled inside, had a single-car garage and was on a safe, tree-lined street. At the time, my mother was in the process of selling her home, and my brother, who is my business partner, took her to look at the place. He knew it well, since he had sold the same unit to a client years before, and had subsequently been the listing agent when they went to sell. The property was listed at $782,000 and sold in about a month for $738,000. What was so surprising is what happened next. By April 2009, in areas of Vancouver, realtors could feel that a change was in the air. Suddenly, as properties began to sell, buyers returned to the market, perhaps emboldened by low interest rates and what seemed to be a new level of affordability.

Apparently, this did not go unnoticed by the purchaser of the aforementioned property or their realtor. Shortly after the sale closed, the new owner put the half-duplex back on the market at a list price of $805,000. By this time, inventory was markedly down and sales were notably up. The property ended up attracting multiple offers and sold for $850,000—THREE MONTHS TO THE DAY of the original purchase. That's a gross profit of $112,000 before closing costs and realtor fees—simply amazing. Even more amazing was the about-face of the market. In a matter of a few months, it had gone from a virtual wasteland, with listings languishing on realtors books, to a fast-paced, multiple-offer situation in many areas. Every area is different, so make sure you evaluate your home's worth based on data relevant to YOU. (There will be more on market conditions in Chapter 11.)

LISTEN TO YOUR REALTOR

Your realtor will be providing the most valuable information regarding the price of your home. When you made the choice of realtor, you hopefully followed my advice and picked the person who knew the neighbourhood, could explain the reasoning behind pricing and didn't seem to be unrealistic. Now, more than ever, you should trust your realtor's advice. Your realtor should be able to answer any of your questions to your satisfaction, and offer examples to support his or her conclusions. **Remember, realtors are the ones who will have the pulse of the market!**

7

"SUBJECT TO SALE" OFFERS AND OTHER "SUBJECT TO" CONDITIONS YOU SHOULD KNOW ABOUT!

In a fast-moving real estate market, you don't often see them. But in balanced or buyer's markets, you do: they're called "Subject-to-Sale" offers, and they are exactly what they sound like. It's an offer to purchase a property based on the condition that the buyer is first able to sell their own home. Buyers will often include a "subject-to-sale" clause in a slower market to ensure they don't get stuck carrying two mortgages at the same time. The buyer is essentially saying to the purchaser, "I'll buy your house, but I've got to sell my place first."

So, what's the big deal about this type of offer, and what are the implications for you? After all, if someone wants to buy your house, then you shouldn't have to worry about a subject-to-sale offer, right? I mean, they'll sell their place and then buy yours! That's the plan, but don't bet on it being as easy and painless as it sounds. Personally, as a realtor, I try to avoid subject-to-sale offers for both buyers and sellers.

FROM THE BUYER'S POINT OF VIEW

Well, the reason buyers include this clause is precisely what I mentioned: to avoid being liable for paying mortgages on two homes at the same time. Who wants to be paying for their new house when they haven't sold their current one yet? But does the subject-to-sale clause really help a buyer in the long run?

Let's suppose it's a buyer's market, meaning there are more people looking to sell properties than there are looking to buy. This usually implies that there is an excess of inventory. Typically, it takes longer for a home to sell under these conditions, no matter how well priced and beautifully presented the property may be. So although you may be champing at the bit to buy a new house, you've got to face the reality that selling your existing home is going to take longer than you'd like.

Subject-to-sale offers usually have a time limit attached to them. For instance, your offer will set out a period of time in which to enter into a firm deal to sell your own home, or the subject-to-sale offer will lapse. In other words, you've got no deal on the new house unless you sell the old one by a certain date. On top of this, any seller's realtor who's worth their salt will include a "time clause," which gives the seller wiggle room. If the seller receives another suitable offer to purchase his house, he may trigger this clause, which will give the original buyer a limited amount of time (often between 24 to 72 hours) to remove the subject-to-sale clause and firm up the contract, or drop out of the running to let the competing offer proceed.

Obviously, there is an advantage for the buyer in all of this, because otherwise what would be the point in writing a subject-to-sale offer in the first place? It means you can go out and find a house you like and can get an offer accepted on it, but you're not stuck with the purchase if your own property doesn't sell. What's not to like?

Well, there's a lot, actually. Ask any realtor and they will tell you you're always going to do better in a purchase without a subject-to-sale clause. After all, money talks, and the fact of the matter is that you don't have any—your money is tied up in your existing home. So, making an offer in this manner means you're dealing at a disadvantage. After all, it's only an offer to buy if your place sells. As far as the seller is concerned, it may mean nothing at all. Bargaining for the dates you want and any other extras may fall on deaf ears. A subject-to-sale clause restricts the seller's ability to sell and move on, so he'll likely be less motivated to negotiate on price, or anything else for that matter.

So you, as the buyer, have less bargaining power. But you also have greater pressure to sell your own home within the specified time. You now have your heart set on a house you love, and you've got (for example) three weeks to sell yours. That means that *you* will have to be very aggressive with your price. You want that other place, so to sell yours quickly may mean accepting a lower price than you had hoped for. So, you had no real bargaining power in the purchase negotiation, and now you have to sell your home fast to realize the deal. To me, that seems like you may have shot yourself in the foot—twice.

I'll cut to the nitty gritty of why this type of offer may not make the most sense in the long run. In a balanced or buyer's market, it will often take longer to sell a home. Depending on market conditions and values, you may be looking to purchase in a price range that ultimately could be out of your reach.

For example, say you spend months looking for a home to purchase, all the while not making an effort to sell your current property. You're looking to move up the property ladder and searching in a price range that is approximately 35% higher than your current home. You place a subject-to-sale offer on the property, but because the seller knows you have to sell in order to purchase, your offer is not considered as strong and your bargaining power is reduced. Now you go to sell your home, and soon realize that the amount you hoped to get for it is just not achievable. But try telling that to your family, who has fallen in love with the new place, which now seems like it may be too expensive, after all. You finally get an offer on your home, and try to renegotiate the purchase price on the home on which you have the subject-to-sale offer, but to no avail. The seller sticks to his price. Did this strategy really work? The good news is, you didn't get stuck with two mortgages.

As difficult as it may seem, I believe that as a buyer you are better off to sell your home first and *then* proceed with finding a home to purchase. There are several reasons why. First of all, you will have the advantage of being able to properly prepare your home for sale, and that includes doing any repairs and updates necessary to make sure it shows well. Secondly, you won't be in a time crunch to sell. You will be able to test the price on the market and make any adjustments deemed appropriate by you and your realtor. The worst-case scenario might be that you're unable to realize a price that would allow you to move to the next level of the property ladder, whether that's up or down. If that's the case, then you won't feel any pressure to do anything, and could remain where you are.

However, let's say that you do get an offer that you're happy with, all goes well with it and that deal firms up. The kicker is that you have to move in nine weeks. Going on the assumption that you're in a buyer's market, you will have a number of properties in your price range to choose from. Again, because there are more sellers than buyers, those sellers will respond to a cash offer much more positively than one with subject-to-sale conditions, precisely because there is cash backing it. A seller who wants or needs to close the sale of his property will be tempted by a cash offer with no conditions, more so than a subject-to-sale offer that is higher. After all, there are no guarantees! On the off chance you're not able to find something suitable to purchase, there is always the option of taking a short-term rental until a home that works for you comes on the market. When that does happen, you'll be in an excellent position to move, and you'll have cash in the bank.

FROM THE SELLER'S POINT OF VIEW

For sellers, I always encourage entertaining a subject-to-sale offer. Sounds like I'm a bit of a hypocrite, right? Well, as I mentioned previously, the seller may have a little more power in the negotiation than he or she might otherwise in a buyer's market. The offer to purchase is based on the sale of the buyer's home, but any offer on a home gives it "desirability," even if the buyer is not in a position to move forward until his current house is sold. Remember, the seller can insert a time clause; this means that if a competing offer is presented, the seller can invoke the clause, and the buyer has a set period of time either to remove the subject-to-sale clause and firm up his offer or drop out entirely and let the new offer proceed. So, by accepting a subject-to-sale offer, the seller is not jeopardizing his ability to entertain other offers and is not locked into that one offer.

Many sellers don't want to waste their time on a subject-to-sale offer, though, and that's understandable. They have to go through the hassle of providing documentation (this could include a property disclosure statement, copy of title and, if the property is a strata, all documentation relating to financials and bylaws). The buyer will most likely contract an inspection (again, another reason why a buyer may not want to proceed with this type of offer: if the offer is bumped, the buyer is out-of-pocket for the cost of an inspection). However, if you do accept a subject-to-sale offer, there are ways to determine whether it has a chance of succeeding.

First of all, the purchase offer will state the address of the property that is to be sold in order to finance the purchase. Your realtor should be able to do a little investigating and give you an idea of what the value of the property is, and whether it has a good chance of selling. A well-priced family home would be ideal, but what if that property is a rundown rental property on a busy street, and your realtor discovers that the buyer plans to list it at a highly inflated price? Well, if that's the case, you might not want to deal with the offer at all.

On several occasions, I've dealt with multiple offers on a property where all the offers were subject-to-sale. This is when you really need to know the saleability of the subject property. In one such instance, I had two offers presented: one was for $15,000 more, but when I discovered where the subject property was and that it carried an inflated asking price, my clients decided to pursue the second offer. It was a good thing they did. It turns out that the subject property represented in the first offer was already listed and the owners said that as soon as they had a firm offer on their place, they would be back to pursue our property. I watched the listing for eight months. The house never sold; in that time. The subject property represented in the second offer that we ended up accepting sold in less than three weeks. The sellers were able to move on, and the house sold, all because a little research that helped push back the initial urge to chase an offer with a better price tag attached.

ALL THE OTHER "SUBJECTS"!

A "subject-to-sale" condition is just one particular type of condition within an offer, but there are many conditions that could be contained in an offer. There are five in particular that I recommend all clients include when they are writing an offer to purchase a property.

Financing

First and foremost, the financing subject is the most important one you can have. This allows you to make an offer on a property based on your ability to, within a certain time frame, secure adequate financing to carry a mortgage on a home. *Never* be foolish enough to think that you will have no problem obtaining financing (and if you don't believe me, it's time to re-read the first chapter in this book, all about mortgage financing!). Don't think that the Donald Trumps of this world don't include a financing clause when they're putting together a real estate deal—they would be fools not to. This clause affords you an "out"—if you find that the financing you can qualify for is too expensive or not plausible, you have the ability to back out of the contract.

When you're qualifying for financing, regardless whether you're pre-approved, most financial institutions will require an appraisal of the subject property. If the bank decides your property is worth what you intend to pay, you should be okay. However, if the lender feels the value is somewhat less than the agreed purchase price, it may leave you high and dry—meaning you may have to find an alternate means of financing or drop the deal altogether. Imagine if you *didn't* have a financing clause, and you had a firm contract to purchase, and yet you had not secured your financing. If you don't complete the deal, you could lose your deposit, and, depending on market conditions, you could lose even more if that property was to re-sell for less than what you offered. The vendor could sue you for the deposit *and* the difference between the two offers.

Inspection

After the financing clause, this should be next on your list of subjects whenever you're writing an offer. You need an inspection clause *even if you are buying an empty lot*. I'm not kidding: even a vacant lot can hold mysteries if you purchase it from an independent seller and not a developer. (And don't give them carte blanche, either.) For instance, there could be soil issues that require environmental clean-up, there could be an underground oil tank that has not been removed—and the list goes on.

Obviously, though, an inspection would usually refer to an existing structure, and you shouldn't buy any property without one. The $500 or so you spend on an inspection could save you hundreds of thousands of dollars. Even brand-new homes should be inspected: who is to say that the furnace venting is correctly installed, or the windows were put in properly or that the electrical is up to current code? You won't know if you don't contract an inspection—and not doing one can mean you may be stuck with a home that desperately requires maintenance. How would you feel if you thought you didn't need to have an inspection, only to find out later the whole roof was rotten, would cost a minimum of $20,000 to replace, and because you passed on an inspection you have no recourse? It's hardly a story you'd want to tell your friends. Inspections will let you know about what kind of maintenance needs to be performed, or more tellingly, what has been ignored. Remember, an inspection cannot uncover every potential or existing problem, but it can often indicate other potential problems that may be lurking. The inspection clause can give you a way to extricate yourself from an offer to purchase, negotiate a price abatement or demand that the problems be fixed.

Property Disclosure Statements

A property disclosure statement (PDS) is just that—a disclosure of information filled out by the vendor of the home that indicates to the best of the vendor's knowledge, the details and, to an extent, the state of repair of the home.

The standard disclosure form is usually a couple of pages long and has many categories—including questions such as "Are you aware of any underground storage tank(s) on the property?" and "Do you know whether the house is on a public water system or uses a well? When an owner lists his or her property with a realtor, they fill out this form, which comes in two formats—one for detached homes and another for strata properties.

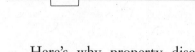
Here's why property disclosure statements are so important and should always be incorporated in the purchase-and-sale agreement as part of the physical contract.

First of all, the PDS actually gives you a great "snapshot" of the property. The owners must fill out this form truthfully and to the best of their abilities, which means there could still be major issues with a property of which the vendor is not aware. However, if a vendor misrepresents the property knowingly, and this can be proved, you as a buyer could have a case against them.

Here's a "for instance"

The vendor has filled in a property disclosure statement that states the roof is approximately 10 years old and has had no leaks. He has owned the house for 12 years. The vendor has said the same to the realtor with whom he listed the property. Upon inspection, the roof does, indeed, seem to be fine (on that beautiful sunny July day you had the inspection done) and there is no water damage visible to the eye. You proceed with the purchase. Four months later, the fall rainstorms have arrived, and water seems to be infiltrating everywhere. In fact, you see signs of previous water leaks and stains brought about by the new ones.

You find out from the neighbor that, yes, the roof is only 10 years old, but the owner had a barrage of problems and that he noticed the vendor had painters and contractors in just before listing the home, to paint the ceilings and perform cosmetic repairs.

Well, looks like you have a case. Unfortunately, inspectors can't find everything—to truly inspect a house, you'd actually have to rip it down to its studs. But in this case, every indication points to that the vendor *knew* there was a problem, went to lengths to cover it up, and did not tell the truth in the disclosure statement. If this disclosure statement is incorporated as *part of the contract* and you can prove the allegation, you may be entitled to claim damages.

This is why many mortgage lenders insist on a PDS—it can sniff out former grow-ops, buried oil storage tanks and a host of other hot issues. In fact, some banks and trusts will simply not finance a property without one.

There are some exceptions to the PDS, such as tenanted properties. Only an owner can fill in a PDS, not a tenant, so if the owner isn't living there, they can't be made to complete one. The same argument is used for estate sales or sales conducted by power of attorney. What typically happens in these cases is that a PDS is initialled and signed, but the page itself is crossed off, to show that the legal owner is not in a position to answer. This can actually help a lot of vendors, as it can relieve them of legal responsibilities in cases where they may be the legal owner or power of attorney, but have no real connection to the property.

Obviously, there are loopholes to property disclosure statements, but they are a very useful tool in the purchase of a home. If you're selling, remember that a "white lie" on a PDS can be very costly.

Title Search

You never know what you might find on a title search, so you'll always want to include a subject regarding a title search in any offer to purchase. Often, the most exciting thing you will find on the title search will be the property's legal description, and if there is a mortgage, the name of the financial institution.

However, you may also find other items on the title. For instance, there could be a builder's lien registered against the property. A builder's lien secures a claim for payment for work done on—or materials supplied to—a construction project or for repairs or renovations made to an existing structure. When a lien is registered in the land title office, it becomes a charge against the title to the land or property involved. So, if you found a couple of builder's liens registered against the property, you would want to research what they were for and the amount owing. Governments can also register liens against a property—usually these are tax liens and they will run with the property. This means that if it's not cleared by the present owner, the new owner would be stuck with the responsibility of paying off the liens. You must perform due diligence to investigate the nature of any lien and to ensure that any liens will be cleared when title is transferred.

Other issues that may surface on a title search are easements and rights-of-way. These usually describe a particular portion of property, and although not visible on the ground, provide an area of access to the holder of the easement or right-of-way. An easement or right-of-way is an agreement that confers on an individual, company or municipality the right to use a landowner's property in some way. While these agreements grant rights, they partially restrict an owner's use of the affected portions of land. Easements and rights-of-way are usually registered on the certificate of title to the property. They remain with the land and are automatically transferred from one owner to another when the land is sold. Easements remain on the title until the holder of the easement discharges their rights from the certificate of title.

Easements are commonly things such as access roads or walkways. If you live on waterfront property, for instance, there may be an easement that allows for public access to the beach. Rights-of-way can often be issued to utility companies. For instance, a gas supplier may have a right-of-way running along the border of your property, and it is usually there for that company to have access for maintenance and inspection. Remember, there are many ways easements and rights-of-way could affect your property. If there is one registered on a property you're interested in, make sure all documents related to it are pulled and fully explained. Easements or rights-of-way are not for the property owner's benefit, so you need to know exactly what that encumbrance is and what it means to the use and enjoyment of the property.

Insurance

Most people don't really think about home insurance; it's just something you get when you call your insurance agent and tell them what you're looking for. However, when you're searching for house insurance, you actually have to make sure your home qualifies. Some companies will not insure certain types of structures; others will, but at a premium. If you're purchasing a home that previously housed a marijuana grow operation, that may make it extremely difficult to obtain insurance, unless the local municipality has re-inspected the property and given it a clean bill of health. Some properties with raised foundations can have difficulties with insurance. Other red flags can be wood-burning stoves (which can be a fire hazard if installed incorrectly) and knob-and-tube wiring. Whatever the case, you should always call your insurance agent armed with all the information you can in regard to the property you want to purchase and make sure there are no issues. Remember, just because the present owner has insurance does not guarantee the same for you. There's always the possibility that the insurer does not have a clear snapshot of the property, and one cannot lay the blame at the feet of the present owner—it could be an unintentional oversight. It may sound like I am putting too much weight on this issue—but remember, if you can't insure the property, you will jeopardize your ability to get a mortgage.

OTHER SUBJECTS

There are many other subject clauses that may apply when purchasing a property. For example, if you're looking at buying a strata (condominium) unit, ensure there is a condition that requires the receipt of relevant information such as strata minutes, the strata plan and bylaws and financials of the condominium corporation. Another example: rural properties may include inspections on wells, septic tanks and fields. In fact, you can include a subject clause for virtually anything that you can think of. Never hesitate to include a subject clause—they are there for your protection. Any seller who takes issue with a reasonable subject clause or condition might have something to hide.

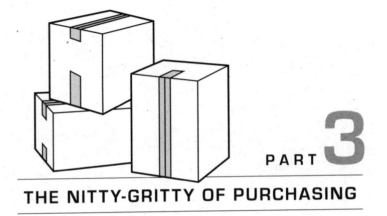

PART 3

THE NITTY-GRITTY OF PURCHASING

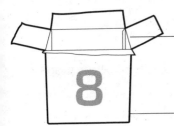

BUYING OR SELLING A STRATA PROPERTY
(Condo or Townhome)

8

For many people, owning a detached home is *not* the dream. Who wants to worry about maintenance when you don't have to? With today's busy lifestyles, many people are looking at condominiums and townhomes as the perfect living arrangement. However, living in a strata property comes with different rules and regulations that you wouldn't have to deal with if you own a home on a freehold lot.

When you own a strata property, you basically "own" your unit plus a share of the common property. Here are basic definitions of the three most common types of strata lots:

1. Strata Units: each strata lot (such as condo or office) is traced out on a strata plan that is filed in the land titles

office. Each strata owner owns a fee-simple title to his or her unit plus a share of the common property (hallways, land, balconies or decks).

2. Strata Duplex or Townhouse: Strata owner owns fee-simple title to a unit, plus has exclusive use of limited common property (balcony, sundecks, yards).

3. Bare Land Strata: Exists where a large parcel of property is divided into strata lots (home sites), and recreation facilities and other amenities are provided in the development as common property.

So, in layman's terms, you're buying your unit which you are entitled to, but as a member of the strata corporation, you, as well as all of the other members of the strata, are responsible for the common property. For instance, in a high-rise building, common property can mean everything from the exterior cladding of the entire building, including roof and balconies, as well as hallways, elevators, parking garage, exercise facilities—you name it.

In most strata properties, you will pay monthly strata fees. (There are exceptions: some properties are non-conforming, meaning they do not pay any maintenance fees or hold any meetings. These occur predominately in free-standing townhomes with no shared walls. If you happen upon a nonconforming strata unit, discuss the implications with your realtor and your mortgage provider to make sure there are no issues). These would go to cover budgetary items such as regular building maintenance, which might include gardening, garbage pick-up, a cleaning service for the common areas; and in many cases the strata fees will include heat and hot water, maybe more. A well-managed strata will also have a contingency fund: basically a rainy day fund for those big-ticket expenses that all homes eventually face, whether it's a new roof, exterior painting and cladding (such as vinyl siding being replaced with Hardy Board, a popular new exterior cover for low-rise condos and townhomes).

BYLAWS

Owning a strata property also means you agree to live by a set of rules and regulations that apply to everyone, so there is a sense of conformity that must go along with ownership. One of the first things you'll want to consider before you even look at a condo or townhome unit are the rules: in general, a listing realtor will be able to tell you the basics before you even go for a visit. But to give you a heads up, some of the most common restrictions cover pet ownership, renting out your unit and ages of the occupants. (When I say "age," some stratas specifically will not allow children to reside on the property; others are 55-plus and designed as a retirement community, though children and grandchildren would be welcome to visit and stay for a period of time, such as a short vacation.)

Those are the big ones, but sometimes it's the minutia that will cause problems in a strata. For instance, do you love to entertain? Make sure you read those bylaws! Here's an example, let's see if you can spot possible bylaw infractions.

Marcia and Rob are thrilled—they've just moved into their condo in an exclusive building they have long admired. Marcia ordered all new furniture, including draperies, and it's all being delivered on Friday—just in time for their big house-warming/Christmas party on Saturday night. Rob had the idea for the theme—it's summer in December! Everyone is to dress in shorts and T-shirts: he's even set up the BBQ and is ready to flip burgers for everyone all night long. Marcia has decorated the windows and balcony with twinkly lights, and by 8:00 p.m. the guests are arriving. The party is a huge success: the first guests to leave don't do so till well after midnight, and many stay late to dance the night away.

So, what bylaws could they have broken? Most people would guess that there would be noise restrictions, and they would most likely be right. But there could be a lot more than that:

- Marcia and Rob ordered new furniture that was to be delivered on Friday. Did they have permission to use the elevator for that purpose? Many stratas require notice and a fee for moving in *or* out, including putting up "bumpers" in the elevator to prevent against damage, and the same with hallways.
- Draperies could be a problem. Some buildings insist they have a white lining; others forbid them altogether as they ruin the uniform look of the complex from the outside (I'm not kidding).
- Many condos will not allow barbeques due to the smoke, smell and potential fire hazard.
- Like the draperies, outside Christmas lights and other decorations to the exterior of the building are often forbidden.

If you've been living in a detached property for the majority of your life, you will definitely want to check the bylaws to make sure you won't find them overly restrictive. Remember, you will not be able to make structural changes to your unit without approval, and that can even include flooring. Some stratas won't permit wood flooring because of the noise transmitted to the units below, although this issue seems to have been solved in recent years with improvements in subflooring. If you are in a townhome, you cannot change the colour of the exterior:

that is a change that has to be agreed upon by the entire strata.

WHAT YOU NEED TO KNOW WHEN BUYING A STRATA

When you buy a condo or any other strata property, you're buying a piece of the strata. Your share in the common property and the size of your unit will be used to calculate your contribution to common expenses. The strata plan will show you the entire strata: you'll see all the units, including yours, in relation to the entire corporation. So, let's say you're considering the purchase of a two-bedroom unit in a low-rise building that has a total of 24 units, or eight per floor. Some of the units in the building are one-bedroom; there are three that have three bedrooms. You should expect that each unit will show a contribution to common expenses (strata fees) according to its size. You should also note any proposed amendments to the strata and changes to the common property. Any changes to a strata plan that are legally binding must be registered on title.

Budget and Annual Expenses

This topic is extremely important. Nobody wants to purchase a strata unit only to find out there's a $15,000 assessment on your unit for a new roof! By carefully reviewing the budget and the annual expenses, you'll be able to tell whether the strata corporation is saving money for big-ticket expenses, scrimping on any maintenance or generally not doing what it should to maintain quality of life for the unit owners. Do not rely on your realtor to read any of the strata documentation for you. What may be fine in the eyes of your realtor may be outside your personal comfort level. Feel free to ask questions to clarify information from your realtor, from the strata itself or from the strata's management company. Ultimately, you make the final decision as to whether you're happy with the strata's finances and budget plans.

You may think that a low monthly strata fee is fantastic, but you might think twice when you realize that short-term gain is going to lead to long-term pain. That low monthly fee could mean that not enough money is being saved for ongoing expenses or big-ticket items. A building that is not properly maintained will become a liability for you when you decide to sell. Remember, the strata must agree to changes, so if you move into a complex that has been lax on upkeep, don't expect to change things. You could be tying your fortunes to a sinking ship. In particular, I always warn people to be cautious if they are purchasing a strata property that has age restrictions, particularly 55-plus. I don't mean to be ageist, but if you're purchasing in a seniors' community and the majority of residents are in their late 70s or older, most of them will be on a set income. That means that big-ticket maintenance items could be deferred, or ignored all together. Just because you want the windows in the building replaced, doesn't mean everyone else does, and those decisions are decided by a vote. It's unlikely that the 87-year-old widow in unit 310 is going to vote "yes" for a $10,000 assessment for new windows and a sliding door to a balcony. She doesn't care!

Strata Minutes

If you want to find out what's really going on day to day in the life of the strata, the strata meeting minutes are the most reliable source of information. Generally, most strata councils will meet at least four to six times a year; depending on the size of the complex, meetings could be more frequent. The strata minutes record all the details of the meetings held, and what subjects were discussed—be it budgets, maintenance or complaints. The complaints part can be the most interesting. It can really be eye opening if you discover through reading the strata minutes that the person living above the unit you plan to purchase has had constant complaints about noise or loud parties. You might want to rethink your plans altogether! Likewise, if there is someone who seems to complain about everyone and everything; that can be an issue too.

The strata minutes will allow you to see the everyday workings of the complex as a whole. Ideally, you'll be reading about boring things such as whether the hedges should be pruned or allowed to grow, or if they plan to change garbage contractors. What can also be telling is what *does not* get addressed: if there's mention of someone complaining of problems with the parking garage, and the following months of strata meetings don't address the issue—well, *that* can be an issue! When reading strata notes, you want to see a clear line of issues that are being brought up, promptly addressed and resolved.

Engineering Reports

An engineering report may or may not be available for the property you may be interested in, but it's always worth requesting to find out if one has been performed. These reports tend to be available mostly in buildings in British Columbia, notably those buildings constructed during the infamous "leaky condo" years. Many of these buildings have been "rain screened" (basically, the skin of the building is peeled off and replaced with a building facade that "breathes"). In a nutshell, the problem with the leaky BC condos was that the building envelope did not let air and moisture flow; consequently; moisture became trapped, literally rotting the building from the inside out. There are buildings that have not been addressed, and to purchase a unit in such a complex could be fraught with hidden costs. An engineer's report would at least provide a snapshot of what kind of action is required to update the facade of the building, and the possible costs. Remember, however, if the building envelope has not been replaced, the strata itself will still need to vote on a course of action.

Again, purchasing a strata property in many ways requires more diligence than purchasing a detached home. Not only are you buying your own residence, but you're acquiring a whole set of business partners, as it were. Make sure you know what you are getting into. READ ALL DOCUMENTS REGARDLESS OF HOW BORING THEY ARE! Like anything, it's "buyer beware" when buying a strata property.

9

NEWLY BUILT HOMES VERSUS RESALE HOMES

One of the biggest decisions many buyers make is whether to purchase a new or resale home. Is there any advantage to a new home, or does older construction make sense?

This can be a personal preference, and I certainly have mine (I like the older construction). But there are reasons you may decide to lean one way or the other.

LOCATION

As we have all heard at least a thousand times, mostly from people like me, location is *key* in real estate. What's the point of building and living in a beautiful home if it's right next to an open-pit mine? And who is the idiot who built that, anyway? Okay, so that's a bit of an exaggeration, but location can often determine the long-term value of a home. It stands to reason that if you find an established neighbourhood with lovely, well-maintained homes and mature landscaping, nice wide streets and close to transportation and shopping, the overwhelming majority of the homes in the area will be previously lived in. Sure, there may be some new homes that would have replaced older properties that were torn down, but in most cases that would be the minority. So, unless you're going to buy something and tear it down and start from scratch, you'll be looking at an older home.

The majority of new builds will often be in newer subdivisions. But here's the catch: those developments tend to be in areas that are not necessarily established yet. It's not like there suddenly will be a new 300-home subdivision landing in the centre of a major city such as Toronto, Halifax or Calgary. New subdivisions are built on the outskirts of the city or town in question. Is this going to be a location that works for you? Is there shopping and good transportation links nearby? Are you going to live in a construction zone? What are the rest of the homes in the neighbourhood going to look like—and is there a building scheme? (Basically, this is an overriding clause on every home to be built in the subdivision. It requires builders to adhere to a certain standard so each new house will fit in with the surrounding properties. Expect restrictions on house colour, roofs, home style and size.) After all, how would you like it if you bought your dream home in a new subdivision, and the lot next door was sold to a guy who puts his dilapidated truck and fifth-wheel trailer on the lot, and plans to leave it there for the next year while he builds his home on weekends? I know I would be less than pleased. Obviously, this can happen in established neighbourhoods too; nobody wants the Aquarian neighbour next door to suddenly become inspired and paint his home bright purple with orange trim. Simply put, though, buying in an established neighbourhood often means you are purchasing a "pre-loved" home, whereas the majority of brand-new homes will be found in new subdivisions in not so established areas. It all comes down to how high up your list the "location" requirement is when you go out house hunting.

FEATURES AND BUDGET!

The style of home you prefer and the features contained within it are a matter of personal taste. It's also a matter of budget! So, what is it you like? Can you not live without vaulted ceilings and an open floor plan? You'll find that you'll probably have better luck finding those types of homes in new neighbourhoods. Looking for something more traditional, with a formal living and dining room? They are definitely more popular in older homes, as they fit the lifestyle of the time they were built. Other things that you often find in new or recently built homes are larger closets, especially in bedrooms, more storage in general and more and larger bathrooms, particularly master ensuites, which seem to get larger the more recently the home was built. Older homes may not have an actual master bathroom at all! On the flip side, if you want more outdoor space, you will typically find that in areas where the neighbourhoods are more established and the homes are older. Remember, when these neighbourhoods, particularly in cities, were designed, land was more plentiful and less expensive. Many (but certainly not all) new subdivisions will showcase homes built on small lots. The entire "bang for your buck" will typically be found in the house itself.

Of course, the curve ball in all of this will be your budget. This can be particularly difficult for those of you who might be just starting a family, and mortgage pre-approval in hand, are heading out to make that big home purchase. If your bottom line is $400,000, you may have two very different choices: 1) Do you go for that home in the established neighbourhood that may be smaller and needs renovation, but has a choice location? Or 2) Do you go further afield, and buy the brand-new home on a small lot that is 45 minutes away? Not an easy choice for many. Some couples I take out house hunting just want something that is "turnkey" and not have to lift a finger, while others are willing to put in a little elbow grease to make a home a better fit for them.

"BUILD" QUALITY

Unfortunately, you cannot fix a poorly built home. Actually, that's not true: you can find yourself a bulldozer. Regardless of the age of the home, the quality of the actual "build" is one of the most important factors to consider in the purchase. It's really all about getting down to the "bones" of the house. The best thing about buying a brand-new property is that you have the opportunity to do some research. First of all, who is the builder? Are they insured and do they offer a warranty with the home? When you're buying from an established builder who has been in business for a period of time, it gives you an opportunity to check out other homes the company previously built in the area.

For instance, you're thinking of buying in a new subdivision being constructed by ABC Developments, and you read in their literature that the firm has been in business for 25 years. I would hope you'd be hopping in the car and driving by those other homes! You'll be looking at generalities, because a builder cannot make a buyer perform ongoing maintenance, but you'll be able to tell shabby construction in a heartbeat. You'll also be able to tell just by walking through a recently completed home. I don't care what the budget is, you will be able to tell immediately if the construction quality is up to snuff. Examine things such as door trims: are they at

90-degree angles and are the finishing nails concealed? For flooring: are there obvious seams in the carpeting? Are there gaps between the floating floor, or do they show signs of buckling? Open cupboards to check inside finishings, and look closely at the quality of the home in general. Sloppy painting, poor installation of items such as light fixtures, switches and electric outlets, and basic substandard detail work is always an indication of overall quality. This is when buyers need to use their head and not their heart. I cannot tell you how many times I have walked into brand new, poorly built homes with buyers, and all they see is the granite countertops and the three-car garage, whereas all I see is cheap cabinetry, a poor plaster job and appalling crown moulding that highlights the uneven ceiling line.

You might think this type of poor construction would be most evident at the entry-level price points, but you'd be wrong. Recently, I took clients to see a brand-new home in a good area, close to the beach. Standing at the street, you could already tell that something was amiss ... it might have been that the chimney was at a slight angle, or maybe the fact that the decorative river rock on that same chimney was missing a couple of stones, showing obvious gaps. But the real fun started once we got in the front door. The heat was on—in fact, you could have grown orchids in the place, it was so hot. While my clients removed their winter coats, I ran around trying to find the thermostat. There wasn't one. I called the listing realtor to let him know. His response? "Crap—not again!" That was just the start of it, though. The hardwood flooring did not match room to room, you could see the walls were off-angle, doors didn't close properly and the list went on and on. My clients looked at me and said, "We love the location, though. Maybe with a lowball offer we could buy the house and fix it!" I answered with a definitive NO. The problem here was that if the home had so many issues that were this obvious, what DIDN'T we see? Though developers have to construct to code and have inspections during the building process, I can tell you horror stories of unscrupulous builders removing insulation, even removing NAILS to use on other properties.

The good news is that there are lots of quality builders out there. They will answer your questions, give references and provide you with samples of the materials they use. They will answer the hard questions and provide the right answers. When you buy a newly built home, on top of an actual inspection which you may still require, you will also have a deficiency list. This is a list you compile on a walk-through prior to closing, in which you look for anything that needs attention. For instance, maybe there is a missing electric socket cover. Or the paint in the living room needs touching up. The list is made and agreed on between the buyer and the builder, as is a timeline for repairs, and you progress from there.

When you purchase an older home, you must remember it was built to the standards of the day, though there may have been many updates since then. Just because a home was built in the 1960s doesn't mean it still has only single-pane windows. A common upgrade that owners make these days is to replace things such as windows with thermal window treatments; older and less efficient furnaces with high-efficiency heating systems—you name it. That's the great thing about renovating too—you can rip out that old, dated kitchen, maybe knock down a wall and voila! Your own custom kitchen! Though there may be parts of the home that are not up to snuff, in many cases, they can be remedied. After all, a home that is lacking sufficient insulation can have more added, and roofs can be replaced. There is a reason that many old neighbourhoods in cities such as Toronto, Montreal and Vancouver feature homes more than 100 years old. They were often built to almost artisan standards, with the kind of scale and quality of woodworking and finishing that's hard to come by these days. Buyers who purchase a home like this in disrepair will take pride in lovingly restoring it and bringing it back to its full glory, but with a modern touch. It breaks my heart when I see homes with that kind of distinction demolished.

Again, like a new home, you'll never know exactly what lies beneath unless you were to tear down the house board by board. But still, inspections will reveal a great deal. When buying a home that might be 40 years old, you need to look at the basics of the structure, and what it would take to bring it up to date. In many cases, that may have already been done! Unfortunately, you most likely won't be able to track down the original builder, but you will be able to judge how the home has stood the test of time. Some homes were built literally to last no more than 30 to 40 years, due to cheap construction practices, while others were designed to stand forever. Whether you buy new or "old," you'll want to purchase a home that falls in the latter category.

OTHER FACTORS

You will pay GST (Goods and Services Tax) on new construction. There are rebates for homes at lower price points. Check with your realtor and mortgage broker for details, but UNLESS THE BUILDER ABSORBS IT, YOU WILL PAY GST ON NEW CONSTRUCTION. You will not pay GST on resale homes. I didn't make the law, so don't start looking for me. In New Brunswick, Quebec, Nova Scotia and Newfoundland and Labrador, new homes are subject to the Harmonized Sales Tax, (HST) meaning not only does the buyer pay GST, but the Provincial Sales

Tax (PST) as well, as the two taxes have been blended. As of this writing, both Ontario and British Columbia are scheduled to bring in the HST as of July 1, 2010. As the cost of newly constructed homes in larger cities in BC and Ontario tend to be higher, many builders and others in the construction and renovation industry are looking at this new tax as having a disastrous affect on new-home sales. Make sure that you factor in these taxes to your purchase cost, along with other closing costs, as this could add tens of thousands of dollars on to the price of a new home.

Unlike an older home, for the most part, new homes come with a warranty on the actual construction. These rules are different from province to province, and there are some loopholes. The timeline that these warranties last will differ too, but they are transferable. Regardless, if you're purchasing a home that was built within the last decade, you should enquire about any warranty, its length and transferability.

When you purchase a home under construction, re-member that your actual possession date may change. Though a good builder will want to deliver the product on time, sometimes factors such as weather, labour and actual delivery of building and finishing materials get in the way. So, if you're purchasing a home that is under construc-tion, be aware that you should always have a back-up plan if it's not ready. If you're supposed to vacate your current home on a certain day and you don't have anywhere to move, you're not going to be a happy camper. You will usually know within a month of the set closing date whether you're going to be on time for your move. If that's not the case, get on the phone and start looking for short-term accommodations! If you're moving to a detached home, you still may be able to store your possessions in a garage, but you won't have that option in a townhome or condo. Organize accordingly!

Again, new build or pre-loved—it's really a matter of personal taste. But one should never go house hunting without considering both. My brother and his wife purchased a home recently that is only one year old. This is contrary to what they have done several times in the past—buying an old home that needs updating, and then remodelling. However, twin three-year-old sons and a 10-year-old daughter, as well as a live-in nanny, a dog and cat, plus two busy careers, meant that this time they let someone else do the work!

HOUSE HUNTING LIST

1. Location, location, location!
2. Price
3. New construction or resale
4. Style of home and exterior design
5. Updates

6. Garden size and fencing
7. Attached or detached?
8. How many stories? (important in both condos and detached homes!)
9. How many bedrooms and bathrooms? Room sizes?
10. Schools and shopping
11. Storage
12. Garage space
13. Features or amenities: i.e., is there air conditioning? Central vacuum? Is there an alarm system? Is it close to parks and recreation?
14. Maintenance costs
15. Fees and/or taxes

10 MARKET CONDITIONS

Oh, to have a crystal ball! I'm sure we all would love that in the real estate market—to be able to predict prices next week or next month, let alone next year. In recent years, we have seen both a rapid upward market, followed by values moving downward, in many cases significantly.

Realtors will often describe conditions in three categories: a buyer's market, a seller's market and a balanced market. If you haven't bought or sold a home in the last five to 10 years, you very well may not have been placing too much importance on the prices of homes in your neighbourhood. The extent of your knowledge might lie in the occasional story on the news either trumpeting rising prices, or shrieking that the sky is falling. Don't base any understanding of the real estate market on the local news:

three minutes is not going to be enough time to analyse how the current market may affect you.

YOUR IMMEDIATE AREA

When you head out to work in the morning or take the dog out for a walk, you probably pass at least two or three homes in your immediate neighbourhood with a "for sale" sign out front. How long is it until you see a "sold" sticker on that sign? If you see it within a month or two of the sign going up, chances are you're living in an area with a fairly buoyant seller's market. If that sticker takes three to six months to appear, it may be more of a balanced market. And if there are more than a few "for sale" signs up in your stomping grounds, and very few sold stickers—or you see those signs go up, then see "reduced" stickers on them, and then those signs disappear ... well, that could mean you are in a buyer's market. Sounds pretty simplistic, but this can be a very accurate gauge as to what is going on close to home. Naturally, there's more to it than that.

Even without the help of your realtor and all the information that he or she can provide, you can do some research to discover how quickly property is changing hands. If you prefer to live in an urban area, there's a good chance there's a local real estate newspaper distributed on a regular basis that shows properties available, advertised by the listing realtors. Look for homes whose descriptions seem to be close in comparison to yours. Look for the price, and then look for any mention of a recent price reduction. If you have access to a month or so of those papers, see if that house has been for sale for a while. You can do the same by monitoring websites such as www.mls.ca. However, the papers will also advertise "sold" listings; when a home sells it will just "drop off" mls.ca, so unless you're checking the site daily, you may miss changes. Don't be afraid to call the realtor and ask what price the home sold for, and how long it was on the market. Also note what type of property seems to be selling well. Do higher end homes seem to sit on the market a long time? Do starter units appear to fly off the shelf? Conversely, what type of listing do you see the most? By this I mean, are there lots of townhomes for sale and few single-family homes? All of this can help you determine just what is selling in your area.

Naturally, your realtor will be able to provide a wealth of information. Realtors have access to "realtor only" sites that can pull up all sorts of information and statistics, including what prices homes were selling for last week, last month, last year and even 10 to 20 years ago. They can access the history of listings, such as the house down the street that may have changed hands three times in 10 years. These sites can provide information such as whether that home was upgraded between sales, shifts in property tax, how long it took to sell each time and whether the price was reduced during the course of the previous listing to encourage a sale. Realtors can also monitor the shift in property inventory. A dearth of active listings can mean that sellers have more leeway in pricing their home aggressively, since there's not a lot of inventory for buyers to choose from. A glut of properties can remove any sense of urgency for buyers, and properties will most likely take longer to sell. Again, that might mean sellers are pricing their homes aggressively in the other direction—bringing their price down to attract a buyer looking to make a deal. In reality, usually the last year of listings and sales will be the basis of feeling out the market, but all that information can be very enlightening.

STATISTICS

You can see how statistics can help shape your perception of your local real estate market. But do be careful how you interpret them, since statistics can be used to support any argument and some just aren't relevant when it comes to determining what's happening where you live. Stats tend to lag a bit when it comes to picking up fast-changing market conditions, so relying on them entirely could cost you some serious coin in the long run. In fact, by our own actions, we can inadvertently affect statistics—and sometimes not in our best interest.

We'll use an example: The Smiths own a home in a nice neighbourhood. The property is tastefully decorated and the kitchen was remodelled within the last seven years. The house sits on a large lot on a quiet, tree-lined street. Whenever the Smiths talk to friends about real estate, they always hear about how the market is so crazy that you can put practically any price on your home, and you'll get multiple offers. Mr. Smith recently retired, and both he and Mrs. Smith are pleased to hear that the home they purchased 20 years ago has appreciated so much. They tell their children that friends have said that their home is worth "X"—a price that even in the hot local market is pushing the boundaries. (As a side note, the friends who are advising them on the list price of their most important asset are *not* realtors.) Their daughter tells them not to get that number stuck in their head, as the market will decide the selling price.

The Smiths decide it's time to sell their home, and against their realtor's advice, they list at the price their friends suggested. Weeks pass, with no offers. After a month, they drop the price, but only marginally. More time passes. They tell their friends about the situation. Eyebrows furrow. Obviously, the market has changed. How else could this be explained? After four months, the Smiths lower their price to what the realtor suggested originally. Suddenly, interest picks up and they receive an excellent offer, which they accept.

So, we've created a statistic that really shouldn't have existed. The property was originally listed at a price that was too high, but cold and dry statistics don't know that. What they show is that the price dropped from where it was originally, and that the property took four months to sell. If you read the statistics and based the market on that information, you would believe that maybe the market was slowing down. But what if they had priced the home properly to start? The statistics might have shown a quick sale, possibly over asking price—and the neighbourhood gossip would *not* be about how the market must be cooling off. Throw in the local news station's three-minute story on a "real estate slowdown" based on those skewed statistics, and suddenly what was a statistic based on a falsehood, might become a reality.

Statistics can give you a snapshot of what has happened up until recently, but can they predict the future?

For many years, a booming provincial economy and speculation in the condominium market in downtown Vancouver played a huge part in the giant spike in prices. Yet, many of these homes would never be lived in by the original purchaser. They were purchased as an investment, with the original buyer intending to sell or "assign" the purchase contract—and at a profit. Here's the example: Jane went downtown and waited overnight for the opportunity to purchase a one-bedroom unit at the "Expensiva," a new high rise that wasn't even going to be breaking ground for six months, and final occupancy was another two years away. She'd heard of all these new developments selling out and she wanted "in" on the bandwagon. Jane knew she had to put down a certain amount, but she wasn't worried. She felt she could "assign" (in essence, sell to someone else who would complete on the sale) her purchase contract within six months and make a cool $50,000, and the building would still just be a hole in the ground.

Statistics seemed to support her plan. But what would happen if interest rates rose, or as we've seen recently, the global economy undergoes a massive upheaval and banks are less willing to give credit? Will the condo market be flooded with people trying to flip their contracts? If they cannot assign these contracts, will they be able to complete on the sale? And if they can't complete, will they lose all their money? With a glut of condos suddenly on the market, will those buyers who do complete their purchase ever recoup their purchase price when they try to sell? Will they even find a buyer? So many questions that statistics cannot answer. Stats show only what *has* happened, and though they can help you *follow* trends, they cannot predict the future.

LOCATION, LOCATION, LOCATION!

We've talked about your immediate neighbourhood, as well as the use of statistics. Now, we need to look at location. By this, I mean where do you currently live? If you live in a community that has an economy built around auto plants and parts manufacturing, where workers are being laid off or losing jobs entirely, chances are you will see more properties for sale, and market values dropping. In such cases, it doesn't matter what your immediate neighbourhood is like, what sales statistics have shown or what the economy is doing otherwise. Cars and car parts and steel that goes into them are the bread and butter of the community and without it, the entire area will suffer.

This can also mean that within a province, or even within an area of a hundred square kilometres, you can see areas in which house prices are moving up, and others where values are declining. For instance, homes in Toronto may be experiencing a rather balanced market, with sales moving well. Toronto is Canada's largest city, with an economy and population that is very diverse. But not too far away in St Catharines and Windsor, house prices are dropping and a buyer's market is in play. Windsor has a large segment of its population reliant on the auto industry, which is facing tough times.

Even your location within a city can affect your price. You can have a stunning home that is the envy of everyone, but if it's in a neighbourhood with a crime problem, that becomes your problem. Houses in areas that seem to be changing to multi-family dwellings can experience value shifts in both directions: upward if their property is deemed suitable for development, and possibly downward for the same reasons. (People looking for a neighbourhood of single-family homes might steer clear.)

Homes in more established neighbourhoods historically tend to do well. Buyers like the mature landscaping and quiet streets. They tend to be free of the noise of construction of new houses; their schools and shopping are well entrenched and the area already has an identity.

Newer developments can sometimes suffer from the "sameness" of the properties. The homes often are variations on a limited amount of exterior styles and interior floor plans, so individuality may be lacking. Another issue can be whether the area is still under construction. You may have a beautiful three-year-old home to sell, but if there are still vacant lots on your block, that might raise a flag with buyers. Why isn't the neighbourhood finished? Will construction be an issue if those lots sell? What kind of houses will be built?

Of course, these are all generalities. Why? Well, because like the chapter's title, it's all about market conditions. Everything mentioned will have an impact on your local market, but it's the combination of this information that will allow you to analyse what's going on. Remember, as we have seen in recent times, the global economy can trump all. A recession or otherwise depressed global markets can lead people to believe it's a bad time to buy or sell. Which leads us to …

PERCEPTION

Sometimes, with all evidence pointing to the contrary, the market in your area can decline, or if you're lucky, can spiral upwards. And it might all be a matter of perception. For instance, say you find out that a brand-new top-of-the line shopping centre is coming to the area. Featuring high end stores and a farmers market on weekends, it's obvious the planners believe that an affluent clientele is there, with more to come. The architects have designed a facade that blends beautifully with the existing community. In this case, obviously, the perception would be that you are living in an "up and coming" neighbourhood—and that can reflect positively on your home and its value.

Conversely, your neighbourhood can be negatively affected by things that are beyond your control. Again, it's all perception. Imagine a nice single-family area with spacious homes, well-manicured lawns and good schools. Then not one, but two homes in the neighbourhood are raided! And one is just two houses away from yours! Nobody ever noticed anything unusual, but it turns out that a major international drug ring and money-laundering gang has been operating out of the two homes. (This might explain the late-night visits and an endless stream of luxury vehicles with tinted

windows parked in the driveway.) Suddenly, news organi-
zations are doing live reports right out front, the papers
have headlines about "the big raid" every day and every new
development in the case brings a spate of new stories. We
can see where this is leading: your home is still in a lovely
neighbourhood with nice homes and manicured lawns, but
you're also next door to that drug and money laundering
operation! Will the criminals be back? Is it safe? Now the
perception of the neighbourhood may be completely different from reality. That can affect market conditions.

Taken to an extreme, an individual home can have a
perception tied to it that might not be attached to its neighbourhood. For example, if a well-publicized death, suicide
or murder(s) happened in the home, regardless of how long
ago, it can have a lasting effect on the home's value. Some
might even call it a latent defect: a latent defect is a fault in
the property that could not have been discovered by a reasonably thorough inspection before the sale. In that case,
it must be declared by the seller prior to sale (presuming
the seller is aware of it), as the information can affect the
actual value of the property, or even the buyers' use and
enjoyment of it. However, on the other hand, the home
may have been the place where someone very famous grew
up, or something historic occurred. That might mean that
even though it is an intangible "benefit," the value may be
increased by it.

There are a lot of factors that can affect market conditions, but the most important thing to remember is that these conditions must be constantly re-evaluated. Every new listing and sale in your target area will reflect on what price your home can command. The neighbourhood itself, the local and provincial economies, statistical analysis and perception—they all play a part. Never think that what is true the day you place your property up for sale automatically applies the next week.

11   WHAT TO LOOK OUT FOR, AND WHAT NOT TO DO!

When you're going out to look at properties, there are some traps that you'll have to look out for. Unfortunately, you can't tell everything by just looking at a home; you have to do some digging. Here are some of the biggies that can cost you a lot of money if you're not on your toes.

FLIPS (GOOD AND BAD ONES)

If you're thinking of purchasing a home with the intent to flip it for a profit, I beg you to reconsider. Actually buying a home with this intention can very quickly cost you thousands of dollars, and could ultimately wipe you out financially.

Unfortunately, the gleam in one's eye that comes from the idea of purchasing a property that is either dated or in disrepair, throwing some money at it for a quick facelift and then selling it for possibly tens of thousands of dollars more, has come from the glut of shows airing on television. Since the heyday of these shows, market conditions have changed in many jurisdictions, although this fact has not stopped people from continuing to attempt to make a quick buck.

First of all, when you purchase a home, as I noted in an earlier chapter, the price of the home is not the total amount you'll spend. Add to that price the fees for a lawyer, insurance, inspection and perhaps surveys, mortgage costs and other closing items. Before you've even put down a nickel to make improvements to the home, you've already added what can be 2% to 3% of the purchase price to the actual cost—maybe even more. I'm going to presume you've had a home inspection carried out, so you will be aware of the maintenance that may need to be performed on the structure. Don't even *think* that you can revamp the inside of a home, and yet not replace a roof that has two years left on it. *Nobody* is going to pay top dollar for a home that has a big-ticket expense looming.

Here's an example for you. A former client of mine was determined to flip houses—back in 2007, when the market was still booming. This client had decided that "flipping" was going to be her new career. Against all advice, both mine and that of her mortgage broker, she forged ahead.

To her credit, she said she knew it was risky, but she felt that she could do it. After a long search in which I talked her out of purchasing several homes in areas she wasn't familiar with, we found her a property in her immediate neighbourhood. The home was a good size, had a suite in it and was in a nice area, with many homes selling into the seven figures. She moved forward and purchased the home. I reminded her that the market was showing early signs of softening, and that she needed to be very judicious in what she did to the property, and spend her money wisely. Since it was late summer and the fall selling market usually flattens out by early November, I told her she needed to act fast or she would be holding the home well into the spring. She was sure she would have it done in three weeks, and had hired a relative to do the work.

This is where the story goes downhill fast. The relative who was doing the renovation injured his shoulder, adding weeks and weeks to the timeline. My client got overly ambitious with the inside of the home, spending too much and personalizing the home to her tastes. She spent a lot reconfiguring the kitchen, yet covered up an existing window with cabinetry: You could still see the window from the outside of the home, yet it was gone as far as the inside was concerned. Money started to run out as she had to hire professionals to finish the job. Finally, ignoring my advice, she did little to improve the outside of the home.

No landscaping, and the back porch remained covered by clear corrugated plastic. The windows hadn't been replaced, but it wasn't essential. What would have helped was to have the windows trimmed with a wood border (this was a west coast contemporary-styled home) to give them a cosmetic boost. The roof was old. Christmas lights remained up. The house had been repainted on the outside, but that was it. Its dated exterior was highlighted only by the fact that the home next door, of a similar age, had an exterior facelift and featured the kind of look that made buyers want to purchase. Problem was, *that* house wasn't for sale. My client's home still had no street appeal.

Then, when it was time to list, my client and I parted ways. She wanted to list at an extremely optimistic price and I wanted her to list considerably lower. There were other issues too, but suffice to say she listed at her much higher price with another realtor. At this point, it was the holiday season, and the market for detached family homes is typically quiet at that time of year. So now, having purchased the home in the late summer, overspending on upgrades and not addressing other structural issues, she had been carrying the property for four months, and the spring market was three months away.

By early 2008, the market was showing signs of a downturn. Prices still remained steady, but there was a bit of fatigue with buyers who were no longer willing to pounce on just any home. I watched as the home languished on the market, with carrying costs adding up month by month. Then, prices began to slip, and as they did, it seemed that my former client was chasing the market downhill. At the same time, the garden was overgrown, and frankly, the house and property looked shabby.

At the time of writing this book, the home has been on the market for more than 1.5 years and the price has dropped more than $160,000. A sale at this point could mean a big loss. I am hopeful for her sake that it sells soon. Unfortunately, this kind of story is not uncommon. There are many homes in neighbourhoods across the country that were the recipients of an attempted flip. Remember, if you do manage to sell and you didn't have the home as your primary residence, among other things, you may have to pay capital gains tax.

The most common mistakes are:

- Doing too much in a neighbourhood that cannot sustain the price you want.
- Doing too little or the wrong thing. For instance, trying to do an inexpensive kitchen renovation in an upscale neighbourhood will cost you more than the reno itself.
- Not budgeting properly.
- Incorporating too much of your own tastes.

- Having an unrealistic timeline.
- Under- or over-estimating the market.
- Spending all your money on things buyers can't see. For example, if you have to spend $10,000 redoing the drain tiles, don't think you'll be rewarded for the expense.

If you're looking to purchase a home and you do your homework, you'll be able to tell a flip. Your realtor will be able to look into the sale history of the property, so if you see that it sold for significantly less just six months prior and it's now done up to the nines, it's probably a flip. There is nothing really wrong with purchasing one; what you are doing is actually rewarding someone else for upgrades you could have done yourself. However, just because the home looks good, doesn't mean it *is* good. As I illustrated, flippers' budgets can fall apart, so maybe the plumbing wasn't done by a professional or other corners were cut. It's imperative that you do a full inspection, and take care to ask for a full list of upgrades. Your realtor should be able to help you estimate what the true costs were to refurbish the home. To a buyer who doesn't know better, a flashily staged flip can lure them into paying too much. Of course, that's what the flipper is counting on!

LATENT DEFECTS

A latent defect is a fault in the property that could not have been discovered by a reasonably thorough inspection before the sale. These can include many issues—for instance, a back yard that floods every spring, a problem foundation, or even if the home had been a crime scene. However, it is the vendor's responsibility to disclose any such defects, as they can materially affect the use and enjoyment of the property. This is the purpose, as mentioned, of a property disclosure statement. The seller should declare any issues with the home. Some items may be considered a material defect by a buyer, but not the seller. For instance, if someone passed away in the home due to natural causes, it would be extremely unlikely for this to be considered a latent defect. But if that same home was the scene of a violent crime or murder in recent years, that very well could be considered a latent defect. The "stigma" surrounding the home could affect the property value. A responsible realtor will not list a home if he or she knows the seller will not disclose a latent defect.

If a latent defect is discovered, there is often a presumption that the seller knew about it. As such, the seller is required to show that he or she could not possibly have known of the defect, rather than the buyer having to show that the seller did know about the defect. However, if it can be shown the seller could not have known about the defect (and was not willfully blind to the possibility), then there is a good possibility that any claim that a buyer might try to put forth won't succeed.

GROW-OPS, METH LABS AND
ALL THINGS ILLEGAL

If the home you're buying or selling once housed an illegal operation, you may be in for a rocky road. (I will presume that our law abiding seller had tenanted the property and was not a party to anything illegal.)

First of all, there's the often total decimation of the interior of the home—and this can be far reaching. Because of the humid environment created in a marijuana grow-op, there's the strong possibility that the walls and ceilings are infested with mould. Depending on how prevalent this problem is, a simple treatment with bleach won't do the trick. In many cases, the drywall must come down completely. Buyers may find unauthorized structural changes to the home that may compromise the integrity of the building, and need to be resolved immediately. And let's not forget illegal wiring—often electric power is actually "stolen"—and makeshift wiring is throughout the house, circumventing approved methods, overloading circuits and creating very real fire hazards. Just getting that sorted out can cost an arm and a leg.

Let's say all this has been done, and it's now it's time to get insurance on your property. Many insurers will simply refuse to insure a home that is a former grow-op, so the vendor/owner must get the municipality or responsibly legal body in for a complete inspection, on their own nickle, to approve the remedies that have been taken and give the home a "clean bill of health." That *still* doesn't guarantee anything; many insurers will take a pass on the property, regardless. If you need a mortgage to purchase the property, you may not be able to get insurance, and without that, you might have to kiss your financing goodbye. This is why many realtors include a subject-to clause in a purchase contract, specifying that insurance is able to be obtained by a certain date, or the contract is void.

The worst part is, you can jump through all these hurdles, and the taint of a grow-op can stick around for years after. In one case, a home owner who had purchased a former grow-op five years previous was being transferred to another city. Unaware that the home's history was an issue, especially since he had, in his opinion, "fixed" the property, the owner never mentioned the former grow operation. His company arranged for the sale of the property, estimates were provided and a price was set. The owner received a dollar amount, the company he worked for assumed the home and listed it with a local realtor. It was only *after* the realtor listed the property that neighbours told him of the home's history. The company that now owned the property had no knowledge of this, as it had not been disclosed by the home owner. Suddenly, the value of the home dropped by more than $300,000 and was really only worth lot value. Yes, it had been nicely renovated, but the stigma remained. And since there was no documentation of any remedies to the property—it was literally, buy at your own risk. (I wonder if the home owner still works for that company!)

The same issues can apply to meth labs. Chemicals used in these illegal operations can make homes inhabitable and downright dangerous. Beyond that, if the property has recently housed illegal activity, you may want to act with even more care. Criminals rarely send out change-of-address cards, and the last thing anyone wants is a bad guy beating down your door because he thinks someone else still lives there. If you have any suspicions and your realtor cannot get answers from the vendor, that's when you'll have to do some snooping in the neighbourhood. This brings us to our next topic.

WHO LIVES NEXT DOOR?

Is the house next door all boarded up, or do you rarely or never see anyone there? It wouldn't be a bad idea to find out why. Nine times out of 10 it's probably because the neighbours are on vacation, or maybe it's a little old lady who rarely ventures out. But it could be something else. The neighbourhood might be great, but the neighbour next door might not be. So, if you can chat up some of the locals (and there's *always* a neighbourhood gossip) you may get some more information. Friends of mine moved from their home after two years when they ended up in a stand-off with their neighbours regarding their teenage sons' constant parties. You'd think that most parents, when informed that their kids are keeping the whole block awake, would do something about it. Unfortunately, these where the dreaded "I'm trying to be cool and be my kids' best friend" type of parents—they were partying with the kids! Something had to give, and my friends decided that it wouldn't be their sanity.

ZONING

How the surrounding area is zoned can have a drastic effect on the property you choose. For instance, will you really want to buy a home if you know that the neighbouring property was zoned for an industrial park? Probably not, but if there's a chance that your property can be subdivided, that could make you some money! It's important to not just check the types of zoning for the property you're interested in, but for the immediate area as well. This can actually help you determine how the neighbourhood may change in the future. Remember, zoning can affect what kind of home you can build, the total square footage allowed, whether you can run a home business and if you can have a secondary suite. *Never assume* that you can make any major changes to a property or how you use it without checking the zoning first. Many a buyer has thought they could open a small business in their basement, and often that's fine within limits. But if you're planning to open a home-based hairdressing business, you might be in for problems. If the zoning doesn't allow it for whatever reason, your business will be *out* of business.

IN CONCLUSION

The real rule of thumb for this chapter is to never assume, always double check and never get in over your head. Don't let anyone answer a question with the words "I'm sure it's fine." Get proof! If you feel you're being pushed into making a decision, back off immediately, and think clearly about what you're doing. Not everything billed as a "deal" *is* a deal. You know the old saying, "If it seems too good to be true, it probably is."

12   THE OFFER, THE NEGOTIATION AND THE CLOSE

Finally, it's that time. Whether you are buying or selling, the contract is going to be the same: it just depends which end of it you're on. In this chapter, we'll address the whole offering procedure and what happens along the way. Deep breaths, everyone; it's more than likely you'll lose your temper during the process at some point, so you might as well know what's coming.

THE OFFER

So, you're a buyer. You've finally found a home that you like, in an area that suits your needs and hopefully at a price point you can live with. You and your realtor meet at your realtor's office to prepare an offer to present to the sellers and their realtor. What does an offer look like? Purchase and sale agreements vary from province to province, but they all include standard information: the property's address (and legal description), price offered, names of the buyer and seller, closing dates and any stipulations of the contract. These stipulations can run from issues like what will be included in the purchase price, to whether the deal is subject to conditions such as an inspection or financing. With the help of your realtor, you decide the price to offer and when you would like to close, what kind of subjects to include. You'll also decide how long the offer will be valid for—for example, until 10 pm the following day, at which point it expires.

Once the offer is signed, your realtor will contact the seller's agent. Realtors will rarely have any direct contact with the actual other party, but will deal directly with the other realtor. Basically, you're sending your prize fighter into the ring, praying you'll get a first-round knockout. Don't get your hopes up. But, for the purposes of this chapter, we'll follow the simple and easy progression, and then we'll get to the horror stories.

The seller, at this point, will be notified by their realtor that a written offer has been received. Let's assume the offer was faxed over and the seller and his realtor sit down to review it. In a deal that all realtors would give their eye-teeth for, we'll say that the seller is happy with the price, deposit, closing dates, inclusions and subjects.

The seller signs the contract and accepts the offer. END OF CHAPTER! In a perfect world, this would be the case, but it very rarely happens. However, that really is, in a nutshell, how simple the initial part of buying and selling can be. Now, let's get to all the things that can slow or even speed up the offer and acceptance process.

THE ACTUAL NEGOTIATION

Probably the hardest part of buying or selling a property is the actual negotiation itself. It's safe to say that most of us assume we'll be fine, and that we'll think with our head and not our hearts, but often all logic goes out the window when it comes to real estate. Sellers want top dollar, buyers want a bargain. In between the two must meet, and that's where your realtor comes in. As I mentioned in an earlier chapter, buying or selling a home is a full-time job. Your realtor is there to do the dirty work, and they enable you to have an "unemotional" representative. Let's put it this way: You want to buy a place, and you absolutely *love* it. In fact, it's the only home you like after six months of looking. Do *you* want to negotiate the deal? Any chance your excitement may show through? I'll pull out the poker analogies now: show no emotion. The same thing for a seller—there's no reason the buyer should know if you're desperate to sell. It undermines your ability to negotiate a good price for your home.

Both buyers and sellers need to remember that everyone wants to come out on top. Truthfully, the best deals are probably those where everyone walks away feeling like they had to give something up—rarely are both sides perfectly happy.

If you've followed my advice from earlier chapters and have done your research on property values, as well as relied on a realtor you can trust to keep you up to date with comparables, you will be able to go into a negotiation armed with the facts. As mentioned, though, sometimes there are scenarios where you may be paying more than the property is worth, such as when a house you love is receiving multiple offers. Or, as a seller, you may find you're receiving offers that are lower than you expected. This could be the sign of a changing real estate market, especially if fuelled by a downturn in the economy (2008-09, anyone?).

There are lots of scenarios that can happen in a negotiation, but I'll touch on a few.

A) *The lowball offer*: Always a nightmare for realtors, this can sometimes be a huge success, or can cause big headaches. It often depends on timing and the type of market you're in. For instance, in a buyer's market, you're more likely to get traction with a low offer, as there are fewer buyers looking to purchase real estate and generally the prices are stagnant or declining. There is an increased chance of getting a low offer accepted if you can close on dates that work for the seller. However, often regardless of the way the winds are blowing market-wise, you may risk insulting and even infuriating the seller.

It's always interesting how clients will want to submit a low offer, but when the shoe is on the other foot and a lowball offer is submitted to them, you'd think they'd be slapped across the face. That's where realtors have to reason with their clients. ALWAYS RESPOND TO A LOWBALL OFFER. Everyone wants a bargain, and you should not penalize the buyer for taking a chance. Do not get all upset and insulted: I know you love your home, but this is business. You will not know how serious the buyer is unless you respond with a counter-offer. Often, you might be surprised.

I recently listed a beautiful home in the low seven-figure range. An offer came in more than $275,000 under the asking price, and the seller blew a gasket. After talking her down off the ceiling, she said there was no point in countering the offer, as these people were, in her opinion, obviously crazy. I insisted that we counter, and sure enough, the buyer ended up coming up in price more than $200,000. The offer did not succeed, only because by the time the negotiation was coming to an end, a competing but higher offer was presented and my seller accepted the second offer. But it proves the point: the buyer was willing to come up in price, and in fact the presence of an active (though not accepted) offer spurred the (successful) second offer to be more aggressive to secure the property.

It's also important to remember that if your home has been on the market a long time with no nibbles, and you have repeatedly ignored statistics as well as your realtor's advice, that lowball offer may not be a lowball offer after all. It might be right on the money, and perhaps the best one you're going to get.

B) *Closing dates*: These are important, as they can determine things such as interim financing and how large a deposit you should take. Let's say you have bitten the bullet and bought another home without first selling your current property. You bought the new home for $650,000, and you're listing your existing home for $495,000. It's a seller's market, so you're feeling relatively confident. You get two offers competing for your house: one for $5,000 over asking price that matches the closing dates for the purchase of your new home, and a second offer that is $18,000 over asking, but closes two months after you have to close on your new home. So, which offer is the one to accept? Probably the first one, even though it's for less money. That's because the second offer means you will technically own two properties for two months, and you will have two mortgage payments and financing charges, taxes and utilities to carry. The inconvenience and the out-of-pocket expenses will eat into the $13,000 difference pretty quickly.

So, what are the respective "closing dates"? There can be three dates given in some contracts, only one in others. But every province, and often individual real estate boards within that province, use different contracts, so you and your realtor should always discuss what applies to you. The closing date is basically the day the buyer pays the seller for the property in question. There may be a separate "possession" date: you might pay for the property on the Monday, but don't take physical possession until two days later to allow the seller to move out. The "adjustment" date could fall on either the closing or the possession date. This refers to "adjusting" certain charges applicable to the property, such as utilities, and taxes. For instance, if you bought a house and the adjustment date was June 15, that would mean that the seller would be responsible for any property taxes or utility charges, or anything else that could be charged to the property, such as strata fees, up until that date. Let's get this clear, though: if these are annual charges like property taxes that are paid once a year, the seller or buyer will be responsible for that percentage of the year of which they owned the property, even if the bill has not yet been issued or paid. These charges are taken care of at your lawyer's or notary's office.

Ideally, you want closing dates that will allow you enough time to perhaps find a new home, and will not cause you a hardship. As I mentioned earlier, a long close may force you to carry two properties, but it might work for you if you want to take your time finding a new home or have other things to tend to. You might get a firm offer to buy your home in May, but you want to close in November. Perhaps you have a summer trip planned, and a longer close means you won't have to worry about changing plans and moving during the summer months. A short close may be ideal too: you want to go on that same trip. Now you can put everything in storage and be footloose and fancy free—you can worry about finding a place to live upon your return!

C) *What's included*: This is where you discuss chattels and fixtures. Chattels are things that are not attached or affixed to the property, but may be negotiated. You may write an offer to purchase a condominium, and within that offer you ask that the washer and dryer, fridge stove and dishwasher are included. You might want the seller to include all the bar stools in the kitchen. It can be anything, but they are negotiable. Never assume things are included that are not actually written in the contract. Fixtures are attached or affixed, or actually growing on the property. A contract will outline what is to be *excluded*. You may want to take the dining-room chandelier and the rhododendron that you planted in the back garden. These must be listed as exclusion in the contract, or you will be legally obligated to leave them behind.

D) *Deposits*: These differ from province to province. In some areas, the deposit is not paid until a deal is made firm, meaning it is subject-free. In other jurisdictions, the standard is to take a deposit on acceptance of an offer. Regardless, deposits should be held in trust. They are held until the completion or termination of the agreement, and are credited towards the purchase price. Again, depending on the jurisdiction, the deposit may incur interest for the buyer. It stands to reason that a large deposit shows intent when purchasing, but it is hardly the only way to judge an offer. However, if someone is offering a low deposit as part of their offer to purchase, it may signal wavering intent.

E) *Subjects*: Subjects are certain conditions that must be met before the agreement becomes firm and binding on both parties. What subjects are or aren't included can help you judge the strength of an offer. A subject-to-sale offer is generally considered weaker that an offer that does not require the buyer to sell his home first. Buyers can write an offer subject to anything—literally. How would you react if you saw this subject attached to an offer presented to you: "Subject to the Buyer, on or before mm/dd/yy, being able to determine from the city bylaws department, whether the Buyer can raise chickens in the garage for the purposes of egg production." It does happen—so imagine if this was one of the subjects in an offer being presented on a home in an urban neighbourhood? It seems obvious this offer would be going nowhere.

Subjects will tie up the property for a certain amount of time in order for the buyer to do their due diligence. However, *sellers* may also have their own subjects to add. For instance, the seller could have a subject inserted saying the sale of their home wouldn't be finalized unless the seller is able to purchase a suitable property by a set date.

Your realtor will advise you to write as "clean" an offer as you can, in the sense that you keep your subjects to a minimum and they be removed in a timely fashion. A typical subject period for a detached home will usually be seven to eight days, perhaps a few days longer for a strata property in order to obtain information from the management company. If you receive an offer from a buyer who has subjects that will not be removed for 30 days, you may have a problem. This means that your property is tied up for that time, and you can only accept offers in a back-up position. Your realtor will always advise against this, with some exceptions. If you're selling a development property that may require re-zoning or has other special needs, you may be faced with a longer subject period. Each case is different, and your realtor will advise you of the best course of action.

OFFERS PRESENTED IN PERSON

In the good old days (from what I am told), offers were presented by the buyer's realtor in person to the seller and the seller's realtor. This was perhaps because, for the most part, we didn't have the benefit of fax machines, scanners, email and cell phones. Ah, for a simpler time! Now it is much rarer to have an offer presented by the other side, so to speak, in person. It can be a benefit in certain circumstances, and can bite you in the tush in others.

If you're planning to write an offer that is significantly lower than asking price, it is generally a good idea *not* to have your realtor present in person, but rather to let the seller's realtor deal with it. Put the shoe on the other foot: if you had listed your home at $600,000 and a realtor presented you with an offer of $450,000, and then proceeded to tell you why your property was overpriced—what would you do? It's one thing to have someone insult you anonymously; it's another entirely to have that person sitting right across from you. Of course, if you've avoided listening to the truth and you've been told by your own realtor that $450,000 is all your property is worth, enjoy that pie in the face, my friend.

However, in a multiple-offer situation, presenting that offer in person may seal the deal. Again, you are the seller, and you have two offers on your property, both buyers offering similar amounts of money and otherwise not many differences in the two contracts. One is faxed over, but the second offer is presented in person by the buyer's realtor. That realtor pleads his client's case: how much the buyer loves the property, how the family can imagine themselves in the home, basically buttering up the seller. This can add a bit of an advantage to the buyer; if the seller feels a connection with the buyer, he may lean towards that offer, even if the conditions and price contained within are slightly less favourable.

It all really depends on the circumstance. Sometimes, the presence of the other realtor can make sellers uncomfortable. Whenever I have an offer presented to a seller in person, I have to coach my seller not to show any emotion; whether it's happiness at a great offer, or the urge to throw a chair across the room over a bad offer. Again, it's like poker: you never know who is bluffing and who's holding all the cards.

MULTIPLE OFFERS

Ah, the dream for all sellers: multiple offers. More common in a seller's market, less so in a balanced or buyer's market, they can complicate the process. Greed can rear

its ugly head, and sellers can sometimes be lured by an offer that might not be all that it's dressed up to be, and in
the long run end up with nothing.

When there's more than one offer on the property, it's
the seller's realtor's obligation to inform all buyers of the
fact that there will be another offer on the property presented. This puts the potential buyer in the position of having to
try to write the most favourable terms possible in order to
secure the property. How does a buyer do this? Well, first
of all, keeping the contract as "clean" as possible, meaning
few, if any, subjects, a competitive price (often more than
the asking price) and closing dates that will be attractive to
the seller. However, it's often the price that sellers look at,
and that can be a problem. You have to be pragmatic when
you're a seller and look at all terms of the contract, as sometimes the offer with the highest price can be the worst of all.

Here's an example. It's a hot market. Let's say you have
a fantastic house for sale, all remodelled, and it hits the
market listed at $499,000—attracting lots of interest. Your
realtor has decided that any offers will be presented on the
following Monday. It's now Wednesday. During this time
prospective buyers can do inspections, look at the title,
the property disclosure statement—basically do their due
diligence.

So, two couples (we'll call them the Smiths and the
Greens) who saw the property on the Thursday, both write

offers. Another couple, the Bakers, who went through an open house on the Saturday, write an offer as well. Which one would you choose? (Remember, all three prospective buyers are aware that they are in a multiple-offer situation, so they want to put their best foot forward.)

The Smiths write a subject-free offer for $515,500. They did their inspection in advance, saw the title and the property disclosure statement and they were pre-approved for their mortgage. They also proposed a closing date that works for you.

The Greens write an offer for $525,000. The only subject they have is a "subject-to-sale," meaning they must sell their home in order to move forward on the purchase of yours. They write completion dates that will work for you, *if* they sell their home.

The Bakers also offer $525,000. However, they have a financing clause, as well as inspection clause in their contract, and they want a longer closing period than you might like.

All three purchase contracts offer similar deposits. For the purposes of this example, we'll say you cannot change any of the three offers—meaning, no counter-offers.

So, which would you accept?

The smart move would be to accept the Smiths' offer, even though it is for $9,500 less than the other two. The reason is simple: an offer in the hand is worth two in the bush—well, you know what I mean. The Smiths' offer is basically a firm deal as presented. If you were to accept the offer, you could immediately consider your home sold. The Greens' offer hangs on them selling their home, and if they don't it, they can't buy yours. So, essentially, what they are saying is "we'd really like to buy your place, but we won't if we don't sell our house." Finally, the Bakers haven't got their financing organized, haven't arranged an inspection and the dates don't work for you. What happens if they find something in the inspection that causes them to want to pull out? Or they can't secure suitable financing? Then you're back to square one. You have to look at all the contingencies in the contract, not just the price, to find the best offer.

All realtors have war stories. This one is true.

In a slowing market, a seller receives two offers on his property that is listed for $899,000. The seller has already purchased a home in another province, where he has accepted a new job. The first offer is for $865,000 and contains the basic subjects: financing, inspection, property disclosure and title search. The second offer is for $880,000, has the same subjects *and* a subject-to-sale clause. Against the advice of the realtor, the seller accepts the second offer.

The would-be buyers list their home and it languishes on the market for four months. In the meantime, other lower offers come in, but the seller refuses to trigger a 48-hour clause, which basically would give notice to the buyers, whose house still hasn't sold, that they must remove all conditions in 48 hours or their offer will be null and void (and thus the seller could move forward). The seller still wants that $880,000, though. The market continues to soften and the buyers decide to let their offer expire. The seller has no offers on the table now and interest in the property is waning. A year later, the seller finally sells his home—for $799,000. Factoring in carrying costs and other expenses, to try and make an extra $15,000 in the sale of his home, the owner lost a lot more.

BACK-UP OFFERS

Here's something to consider if you're lucky enough to be in a position to have multiple offers on your property: the back-up offer. It's exactly what it sounds like. If the first offer accepted falls through (if, for example, it was conditional on financing that didn't come through), then the back-up offer would come into effect. It doesn't even have to apply to multiple-offer situations; obviously, if you and your realtor feel the conditional offer you're dealing with is looking shaky and you aren't sure the buyers will remove their subjects, you don't have to wait for the conditional deal to fall apart. The back-up offer would be written to reflect that it only became valid should the conditions on the first offer not be removed. It's a good idea as a buyer in a hot market to consider this strategy: if your back-up offer is accepted and the initial accepted offer falls apart, you don't have to battle it out again with other interested parties. Of course, you do have to wait to see what happens, but it can be a calculated risk to your benefit.

DUAL AGENCY

A dual agent is a real estate broker or salesperson who acts as agent for both the seller and the buyer in the same transaction. Both buyer and seller are the agent's clients. It's a tricky road to walk as a dual agent, in that the realtor cannot reveal anything the buyer has told him, and the same applies to the seller. If your realtor is going to represent both buyer and seller, he or she must disclose this information to both sides. In most cases, it won't be a problem. Often, a buyer feels he might get a better deal if he uses the same agent the seller has listed his property with, but a good realtor will not allow either side to influence him or her. I mention this here as a dual-agency situation should not affect your ability to negotiate—and if you feel uncomfortable, you can refuse the arrangement.

Again, the thing to remember when you negotiate the purchase and sale contract, regardless of what side of the table you're on, is try to keep a cool head. Know what your limits are, and be prepared to walk away if necessary.

What you will most likely find is something that we realtors know well: it's always the last couple of dollars and the smallest details that torpedo a deal. I've seen multi-million-dollar deals go sideways over such things as a $500 walkway repair or the inclusion of a refrigerator. But the most common thorn is the last $5,000 to $10,000. It doesn't matter how big the price tag is, it is the last few numbers on the offer that seem to count. Try to be realistic and look at the larger picture. That will make the whole process so much easier to manage.

ASSIGNMENT OF CONTRACTS, AND WHAT IT MEANS TO YOU

This is a pretty new topic in Canadian real estate transactions, but it bears discussing because depending on what part you have in the transaction, it can be a great opportunity or a grave mistake.

We've seen assignments lately in the condo markets, specifically in the larger cities with hot real estate markets for high-rise buildings. I'm sure you've seen it—that sign on a downtown vacant lot promising the next best glorious high rise, complete with every possible amenity known to mankind, scheduled to break ground in the coming months, with pre-sales occurring at a certain time. In recent years, that's been the timeline: The developer would literally sell condos that hadn't been built yet and probably wouldn't be built and ready for occupancy for several more years. However, when real estate values began to climb, a sub market was created—assigning contracts.

What is it? Well, let's say I bought a new unit at the (yet to be built) "Expensiva," Vancouver's newest and best condo high-rise, in the fall of 2005, at the height of the condo boom. I purchased my unit for $239,000, made a down payment and looked forward to completion in the spring of 2008. But a funny thing happened: I decided to travel for a year and realized that I didn't really want my condo after all. So, what do I do? What a lot of others did— assign my contract. Of course, my motives may have been innocent enough, but in many areas investors purchased these pre-sale units with the sole motive of being able to assign the contracts, for a generous profit, later down the line.

Most contract assignments require three factors: the (written) permission of the developer to assign the con- tract in the first place (which may require a fee paid to the developer); the original buyer and the second buyer, (who becomes the assignee) who wishes to purchase the contract for the condo and complete the sale, thus becom- ing the registered owner. It's a complicated process, and depending on the developer and prior deposits involved, will require a lot of paperwork and a lawyer or notary to wade through the fine print.

In some instances, the developer may refuse to allow assignments of contracts: if you're considering purchasing an unbuilt condo, make sure you scour the fine print. If the delivery of that condo is three years out, and you cannot assign the contract, if your personal situation changes drastically you could find yourself in hot water.

But, what if you do assign that contract?

The problem is, though you think you have "sold" that unfinished condominium, you're still legally on the hook if the person that you assigned the contract to is unable to complete the transaction. You see, the initial contract was made between you as the purchaser, and the developer. If for some reason there's a problem along the way, it could be you as the original buyer that the developer will turn to for damages.

Here lies the rub. In some cases, contracts have been assigned several times before the property is completed. So, imagine that unit I bought for $239,000 and assigned for a nice little profit (let's say assigned for $299,000), was reassigned again, this time for $389,000. Meanwhile, I've gone off on my travels, having long forgotten about the condo unit. Spring of 2008 arrives, and the building is a bit late in finishing, but they expect occupancy for September—and then things go horribly sideways. As we all know all too well, September 2008 was when the global economy took a nosedive—well, I'll say it—into the toilet. The person who was now the holder of that assigned contract loses their job and with that their financing. This means they will be unable to complete on the purchase of that condo that I bought all the way back in the fall of 2005. This could mean that I am now on the hook to complete on a condominium that I thought I had sold! Sounds scary? Well it does happen, so regardless of what side of an assignment transaction you're on, make sure you're fully aware of any liabilities you may incur in case something goes awry.

Sometimes, even more bizarre issues can come into play. There have been instances where owners of development land have sold their properties, but with a completion date that was a fair way off—say 18 months to two years. Once the deal is firm (but hasn't closed), the purchaser has assigned that contract to another speculator for a handsome profit, and then that buyer did the same thing. Now, all of these people took profits along the way. What would happen if the original owner caught wind of this, was able to say that they were taken advantage of by unscrupulous realtors, lawyers or whomever, and refused to complete the sale? What happens to the money trail? It turns out that all these buyers could have paid for nothing—and who does the end holder of the contract go to for his money? After all, he paid a premium to purchase the RIGHT to complete, but now he has no land to buy!

Before these kinds of assignments occurred, though, the most common type of assignment was often between family or friends. For instance, let's imagine you wrote a contract of purchase and sale for a house in your neighbourhood. You love the home and are very excited about moving in—but it turns out that a family looking for a home in that area missed their chance at the house, and they desperately want to purchase it. They track you down and offer you a nice little bonus if you assign the contract to them, and you decide to do it. Again, this would be a transaction handled by your lawyer or notary, as it's beyond (in most cases) the scope of your realtor.

You might think, why not just sell them the house? There's one obvious reason: to avoid paying closing costs. If you follow through on the purchase, you will pay your province's closing costs, as well as any financing costs that may occur, taxes owing, utilities, you name it. The assignment of the contract passes on that responsibility, so title on the property is not transferred twice.

Assignment of contracts isn't that common. However, for many looking to purchase a condo in yet unfinished buildings, it is a viable way to get into a building they might have missed out on previously. As mentioned, though, there are many twists in this road. Generally, you will not find assignments on mls.ca, as only the owner can sign a listing contract and technically the developer is the owner until completion. So, you have to find them—and that means that it's usually a private transaction, without the advice of a realtor. Again, exercise caution.

13 THE HOME INSPECTION—DON'T BUY A HOME WITHOUT ONE!

I will never let a client purchase a home without a home inspection. The mere suggestion of not getting a home inspected is kind of like volunteering to empty your savings account and potentially take that money and use it to line a bird cage. Why would you willingly hand over possibly hundreds of thousands of dollars to purchase home and not spend a couple hundred bucks to make sure it will still be standing a year from now? A home inspection can literally save you hundreds to thousands of dollars—and maybe save you from buying a money pit altogether. Whether it's the discovery of extensive mould, a bad roof or an improperly installed wood stove, the things you don't know about before closing the sale are going to be the ones that cost you the most.

WHAT AN INSPECTION CAN AND CANNOT DO

The perfect inspection, one that would find everything that could possibly be discovered, would require having to tear down the entire house. I think we can all agree that just isn't practical. However, a thorough inspection provides vital information about plumbing and wiring, heating and cooling systems, and affords an overall assessment of the quality of the structure as a whole. Upon completion, most inspectors will hand you a full report that includes a summary of everything inspected in the property, from plumbing to foundation, wiring to roofing. This report is a superb reference tool, since there's no way you'll be able to remember all the information otherwise. This is important, as a lot of little issues can lead up to some big bills, and you'll want to know what the costs will be before you continue with the purchase.

For the most part, the current owners will be able to provide some information about the home that may not be outlined in a property disclosure statement (PDS)—for instance, when the furnace was installed, the age of the hot water tank and even the age of the appliances. The inspector will be the one who takes it to the next level. For example, the roof may be 20 years old, but if it's a steel roof, then it's got lots of life left. An inexpensive asphalt shingle roof may last only 10 to 15 years, so if the PDS states that the roof is already seven years old, it may be a consideration for you.

An inspector will be able to tell you whether the home has adequate insulation (and if there are any issues with asbestos), or if there has been any rodent or bug infestation. (And, to a point, determine whether the bugs are still active.) For purchasers of rural or vacation properties, separate inspections for properties with septic tanks instead of sewer hook-ups are common, because a faulty or inadequate septic system can cost thousands of dollars to upgrade or repair.

What an inspection cannot reveal is latent defects. For example, if the home is built in an area that has water-pooling issues in the front yard every spring that result in a damp basement, or poor drainage for the garden. If you purchase the home in the late summer, there may be no way an inspection will pick these up—and chances are, a home inspector would not be able to comment on land drainage anyway. If the seller is aware of any latent defects, they must legally disclose them on the property disclosure statement. If a latent defect is discovered after the fact, it's usually the seller's responsibility to prove he was unaware of the issue.

Again, though an inspection can tell you a lot about wiring and plumbing, inspectors cannot look behind the drywall and lift up floors and foundations, so there's a limit to the information they can provide. They are, however, able to tell you if they see symptoms of a larger problem, perhaps water stains or dampness, or in the case of wiring, shorts or below standard service.

Even condos and townhomes should be inspected. Just because the outer shell of the building may be considered common property does not mean you're not responsible for carrying out this necessary due diligence. Let's say the inspector you hire goes up on the roof of the strata property you want to purchase, and determines that there are obvious problems such as a bad patch job or ageing. If you find there is no money in the strata's budget for a new roof and very little in the emergency contingency fund, you could be in for an assessment for a new roof in the near future. That's something *you* may not have budgeted for.

It's important to remember that the home inspection is a snapshot of the home you wish to purchase on the day the inspection takes place. For instance, the washer and dryer may be in working order at the time, and then break down three weeks after you close on the house. Whose problem is it? Most likely it's yours. Usually appliance warranties are not transferable to a new owner, and the former owner can claim that the washer and dryer were working just fine when they left. Chances are, they're being truthful. Things happen. The roof of my home was only three years old when I ended up with water dripping on my forehead while sitting on the couch watching TV. It turns out it was a seal around the chimney, but it was my responsibility, even though I had only lived there a short time. There was no way the previous owner or the inspector could have foreseen that.

Also note that you should make every effort to be present for your inspection. This is when your inspector will walk you through what he or she has found, what maintenance issues may need to be addressed and anything else that affects the structure of the property. It's difficult to get a handle on any issues unless you have seen the problems first-hand and had them explained to you. The buyer's realtor will often be on hand for at least part of the inspection, but the inspector is independent of the realtor; the realtor can help you renegotiate the price if major inadequacies arise, but most realtors are not qualified to give an opinion on the outcome of an inspection.

A typical inspection can vary in price and will often be based on the square footage of the home. As I mentioned, you can contract other inspections as well, such as those that cover septic systems, water wells and even soil. What are those? Well, the septic inspection is self explanatory, but a well inspection will tell a buyer whether there's an adequate supply of water, usually measured as litres of water flowing per minute. A water inspection isn't an inspection per se; generally samples of the well water are taken to determine if the water is drinkable. Some water may be fine for irrigating crops or for animals, but may have levels of certain substances, such as arsenic, that make it unfit for human consumption without filtration. If it turns out that a water filtration system is needed, it can add thousands to the cost of purchasing the home.

For a home inspection, though, expect to spend anywhere between $400 and up to $1,000. But don't be fooled into thinking the most expensive one is the best.

THE QUALIFICATIONS OF AN INSPECTOR

At the time this book goes to press, the only province that requires inspectors to be licensed is British Columbia. Though there are certification programs in other provinces that require home inspectors have a level of competency, these provinces and territories currently do not mandate licensing. But regardless of whether you live in BC or elsewhere, you need to do a bit of research when you hire a home inspector.

Generally, the best recommendation is a reference from friends or family who were satisfied with the report they received and the professionalism of the inspector. A good, experienced inspector will be able to explain issues easily and in a way that makes sense to the buyer, and provide a written report upon completion. The inspector should have credentials, obviously—many have worked for years in the construction industry and have taken that knowledge, with extra training, and moved into the home inspection field. Ask for references, qualifications and length of time in the business. Find out if the inspection company is a member of the Better Business Bureau. Your realtor will also be able to provide a list of inspectors who work in the neighbourhood. An ethical realtor will always provide more than one name, to give you the opportunity to choose who you feel comfortable with.

Many people think they can save a bit of money and get a friend to inspect a property for them. You know, the "I built the tree fort in the back yard for the kids, so sure, I can inspect a 2,500-square-foot home" guy. DON'T DO IT! This is basically the same as not having an inspection at all. Always have an independent inspection: do not rely on a report provided by the seller or an inspection conducted several months earlier. I had a client write a subject-to-sale offer on a property that ultimately did not go through, but the client did have the house inspected. It came off the market a month later, and was then re-listed. At that point, *another* client of mine purchased the property, but wanted to see if we could obtain the previous inspection and thus save some money. I told her it was not a good idea; the report was five months old, and literally anything that would affect the house could have happened in the interim.

Obviously, there is always the risk of ending up with an incompetent inspector, but there's a flip side to that one:

the deal killers. Realtors will tell you about these inspectors—there's a few in every city, and they will often boast they can fail any house in an inspection. However, a home can only be judged fairly in comparison to the homes built in that era and in that price range. You cannot compare a home built for $300 a square foot at 2010 standards to a home built in the 1960s to what the building code was at the time, and not updated in 20 years. Obviously, the latter will probably need new windows, maybe exterior cladding and possibly a new roof. Insulation may be substandard. But that doesn't "fail" a house; these are items that will be mentioned in the report and will most likely have been factored into the sale price.

Nope, I believe the deal killer inspector has an ulterior motive: to make more money. I had a property listed, which received a subject to sale offer which my sellers accepted. Soon after, our prospective buyers received an offer on *their* home. It was a cute old-timer they had lovingly restored, including new windows and roof, all new flooring, new drain tiles, a brand-new kitchen and bathrooms. All the work had been done by professionals and passed by the city. The other realtor phoned me to say all was progressing well, and the inspection on that home was later in the week. That's when I got the call: they had been visited by one of the city's infamous deal killers. He told the buyers that the home was a tear-down!

So how is this inspector making more money? Well, those buyers will now move on to try and find another home, and that means they'll need another inspection. And who will they choose to do the inspection? The guy that think saved them from "making a terrible mistake." Ta-da! Pay cheque number *two*. Certainly, homes fail inspections for valid reasons all the time. However, our prospective buyers contracted two other inspectors to check their home, and neither could come up with any reason why the home would fail. Simply put, a home inspection should be reasonable, and not statements such as "there's a broken light bulb in the furnace room, which leads me to believe that the owners are covering up maintenance issues." Sometimes a burnt-out light bulb is just a burnt-out light bulb!

YOUR INSPECTION AS A BARGAINING TOOL

Sometimes, an inspection can reveal a major issue that even the home owner was unaware of but the buyer wants to proceed with the purchase. However, for the deal to go through, the buyer may ask for (or the seller may volunteer) an abatement, or renegotiation on price. If the seller believed the roof was good for another five years, but the buyer's inspection shows there is water erosion and missing shingles and the roof is on its last legs, revisiting the purchase price can sometimes save a sale. If you're buying a home and the inspection reveals big problems, don't be afraid to negotiate. The seller has the right to say no, but you might as well try! Your success may hinge on the type of market you're purchasing in: a hot seller's market will obviously be to the home owner's advantage; the opposite is true in a buyer's market.

Finally, hold on tight to that inspection report—you'll be referring to it when you move in to your home. It will provide information such as what work should be done soon, what maintenance issues to watch out for and what need to be tended to immediately. An inspection is basically like taking the "pulse" of the home—and it's your job to see that it still has one in the years to come.

14 BETWEEN THE FIRM DEAL AND THE MOVE-IN DATE

Once you've successfully negotiated and finalized the purchase of your new home, the *actual work* really begins. That's right friends, no time to pat yourself on the back quite yet. There is so much that still needs to be addressed, and chances are you'll only have a couple months to get everything done. Whatever you do, don't delay in making all the necessary arrangements; it could affect not just your move, but your pocketbook.

LAWYER OR NOTARY

One of the first phone calls you should make after the deal is firm is to a lawyer or notary who specializes in home conveyance. Your realtor should be able to give you a list of candidates who work in your area. These lawyers or notaries take care of the actual process of the purchase or sale: they arrange for the transfer of funds in exchange for title, and receive and handle mortgage documents and the discharge of any mortgages being paid out. They make sure that any liens on title are cleared, and that taxes and any other fees owing are up to date at the time of the property's legal transfer.

The actual completion, or sale finalization process, differs from province to province, so if you're moving from Alberta to New Brunswick you will not be using your Alberta lawyer to complete the purchase in New Brunswick since the laws are different.

Though everyone loves a bargain, in this kind of transaction, the best deal may be the most costly. Documents not properly prepared can delay the completion on your property, and possibly impact your possession date if funds and title have not been transferred. That could lead to you driving aimlessly in circles in the moving van! Be sure to ask your lawyer or notary if property conveyance is something they perform on a regular basis. Your friend the lawyer who primarily handles divorce cases or accident claims probably isn't the wisest choice to handle your purchase or sale. A well-run office that specializes in this service will be your better bet.

Several years ago, I had clients who sold their home and purchased a brand-new townhome. Unfortunately, the sale of their home and purchase of the new place were to go through on the same day—called a "double completion." It's something we realtors like to avoid but sometimes is necessary. Though I had given them a list of choices for the conveyance who used electronic transfer (in BC title and fund transfer can be done this way), they opted to use a friend who was a notary. Unfortunately, he was a part-time notary; he actually worked full time with one of my clients.

When closing day came, he was driving around with paperwork and visiting my clients for coffee, all while two deals were hanging in the balance. Because he wasn't set up for electronic transfer (mainly because this was a sideline for him), he only got the sale of the original property through the title office, and so was unable to complete the purchase. My clients had packed up their home in preparation to move into the new townhome that evening, but the developers wouldn't hand over the keys since they hadn't been paid. On top of that, the notary told them it was all *my* fault. I didn't find out till the next day: I had gone by the day the deal was supposed to complete with a housewarming gift, but my clients weren't there and weren't answering their cell phone. That's when I found out the blame had been placed squarely on my shoulders, by a notary I had told them was probably not capable of executing a double completion. They may have saved a couple hundred dollars in using this person, but clearly it cost them. Had they used a lawyer or notary who used electronic transfer, this wouldn't have happened. They were able to complete the purchase of their new home the next day, but had to keep all their possessions locked up in a moving truck for an extra night. (The clients continued to blame me; I did send a letter to the notary threatening legal action if he continued to slander me.)

MORTGAGE DOCUMENTS

Every jurisdiction operates differently, so you may be signing mortgage documents at your lawyer's office or with your bank or mortgage broker. But in the weeks leading up to finalizing your purchase, you'll be deciding what terms you want. This would include the frequency of payments (monthly, bi-weekly, weekly), the term of the mortgage, fixed or variable rate and the length of the amortization. (Amortization is the length of time you will be paying off the debt. In Canada, the longest amortization period is now 35 years, with most conventional mortgages having a term of 15 to 25 years.) Most of this will have been decided when you were pre-approved for a mortgage, but this is when these terms need to be finalized, so don't take anything for granted. In order for documents to be prepared in time, make sure you call your bank or mortgage broker *as soon as you have an accepted offer* on the property you plan to purchase. You or your realtor should fax a copy of the contract of purchase and sale, which enables the financial institution to study the contract and order a bank appraisal of the property. It also makes sure the contract is acceptable to the mortgage provider. As stated in a previous chapter, this is the reason for having a condition in the offer that outlines financing.

INSURANCE

As soon as you have a firm deal on the property that you have purchased, make sure that you arrange for home owners insurance. In many cases, depending on the type of property you are purchasing, this may have been a condition that had to be met in order for the deal to become firm. If this is the case, you will have already spoken to your insurance agent, and will have answered some basic questions such as the age of the home, the heating system, type of construction, etc. Many of your insurance agent's questions can be answered by the spec sheet provided by the listing realtor, but chances are more information will need to be gathered. Make sure that you attend to these details well in advance: homes with alarms will often get a discount on insurance, while some types of homes may be subject a higher premium based on anything from the age of the home, to the distance from a fire hall or fire hydrant. Regardless, insurance must be in place as of

12:01 a.m. (in most cases) on the closing date REGARD-LESS of whether you take physical possession on that day. Check with your insurance agent for more details.

FIND A MOVER—NOW!

This is an absolute must—and make sure you don't delay on this one. If you wait until close to the moving day, you may be out of luck entirely and might end up scrambling to rent a truck and do it yourself. Not that moving yourself is a bad thing. Just remember, that comes with hidden costs. You may be saving money on hired movers, but if you're going to rely on friends, you may have no insurance if something gets damaged or destroyed. It most likely will take longer to get the job done, and chances are you will have to feed them (and buy the beer, too). But the worst part is, when one of your friends moves, you'll be obligated to return the favor. FRIENDS DON'T HELP FRIENDS MOVE. Trust me on this one. I understand that sometimes it cannot be avoided, but the savings in stress, time and possible damages is worth every penny.

I've seen what happens when people underestimate the time and expense in moving. Like the seller who is supposed to be out by noon and hasn't even emptied the fridge yet—while the irate buyer sits out front with a loaded truck. If you're supposed to hand over the keys at noon, you should be aiming to be out and the home cleaned and ready for the new owners by 9:00 that morning at the latest. Depending on the size of the home that you're packing up, you should begin a week in advance (unless you have professional packers too—in which case, lucky you!) Most moving companies will provide boxes for a small fee, but you might be able to round some up at local stores. Keep in mind that the end of the month is the most popular time to move, so if your moving dates are at that time, you will need to book your movers as soon as possible.

You should NOT still be packing on the day you are supposed to be out of the house. If fact, your movers should be booked to arrive and start loading your possessions about two to three hours before you get legal possession of the home you have purchased (assuming it's a local move). Generally, you will probably have legal possession of the home you've sold for a period of time that overlaps the purchase, so this gives you ample time get out and clean up behind you. I always recommend that my clients hire a professional maid service to do the final cleaning of their old place. Otherwise, you'll be up all night wiping out the refrigerator and scrubbing the bathtubs, when you could be unpacking in your new home. Chances are you'll be pressed for time, and the time savings is worth the extra cost.

When hiring a mover, make sure you have good references. There are the national chains, and they tend to be at the higher end of the price range. Local companies can provide excellent service, but again, there are some less reputable ones. Check references and the Better Business Bureau. Make sure the mover you hire is bonded and insured. Get an estimate as to how much the move will cost; clients are often surprised at just how much stuff they own, and having a representative from the moving company provide a written estimate will eliminate ugly surprises. Ask about any "hidden" fees—sometimes, there are extra charges for heavy items or setting up beds. Make sure you're clear as to exactly what you expect. If you only want the movers to literally load at one end and unload at the other, and you don't need help unpacking, make that clear. If you're signing a contract, read the fine print!

INCIDENTALS

There are lots of little things that may not occur to you at the time but that you need to consider before your moving date. Here are some of the top points you might need to deal with:

1. If you're moving from a home and taking the alarm system with you, you should call your alarm provider immediately and make arrangements. Every company has different requirements: some will move the hardware, others won't. I can't think of a

company that will not allow the new owner to assume the system and its contract (if any), but if the buyer doesn't wish to assume it, you may be responsible. Conversely, if you want to have a new system installed at your new property, don't wait till moving day to make the appointment; call immediately and book a time.

2. It's always a good idea to have your door locks re-keyed when you move in to a new home. This is not to cast any suspicion on the previous owner, but they may have extra keys floating around that aren't accounted for. In some cases, unscrupulous movers have used keys to break into homes weeks after the buyer has moved in. (After all, that mover would know exactly what valuables you have in the first place.) Regardless, for your own peace of mind, book a locksmith to come by and re-key all the external doors. It doesn't require any new locks, just some time and minor expense. It's worth it.

3. If you're having any painting or flooring done or any renovations at all, get on it! Good plumbers, contractors, painters and electricians are always in high demand. If you're ordering product such as carpet or wood flooring, it may not be in stock and take weeks to arrive. If you're going to be undertaking a major renovation, bring your contractor to the inspection

when you're in the process of purchasing. Ask your realtor to write into the terms of the contact that you will be able to visit the property, with appropriate notice, on a certain number of occasions prior to closing. Get organized and book your trades people immediately.

4. If you have pets, I strongly advise making arrangements for them to be looked after by a friend, or kennelled at a vet or a boarding service for the days around the move. Cats and dogs can get very stressed by moving, and sadly many can be lost forever in the process. Cats are easily spooked, and may get loose and find themselves in a strange environment. Dogs may react the same way, but throw in things like barking, chewing and marking—or even possibly nipping someone they don't know in a fearful reaction—and it's a bad situation for all. Your pet will be a lot happier, and you'll have less to worry about if they're in a safe, friendly place while you move. Ideally, you can pick them up after all the chaos has settled down, and your home resembles something they recognize, with familiar furniture and smells.

WHAT YOUR REALTOR CAN DO FOR YOU

Your realtor can provide you with assistance and refer you to lawyers or notaries and even contractors. But for all intents and purposes, you are responsible for all the little things listed above. One thing the realtor will definitely organize is the key exchange. The seller's realtor and the buyer's agent will make arrangements to pick up keys and any alarm codes or key fobs and garage door remotes. In most cases, the realtor who represented you in the purchase will be the one handing over all these items. Most will also perform a walk-through of the home as well, to make sure all is in good order. (Just a note: if the property you're purchasing is particularly dirty or messy, inside or out, you might want to include a clause in the purchase and sale contract requiring that all debris be removed and the home be delivered in clean condition. If you are particularly concerned, you may include a dollar amount as a "holdback": if the clause is not honoured, that amount is not paid to the seller. That way you have money that's not coming out of your pocket to pay for any clean-up required.)

There are lots of things to consider when getting ready to move. Don't put anything off—you may not be able to book people for the time frame you need if you wait. Having everything organized with plenty of time to spare will make the whole experience a lot more pleasant.

15 ADDING A MORTGAGE HELPER TO YOUR HOME

It's a common question: can I add a suite to my home, whether it is a basement apartment or a garage conversion, to help with my mortgage? What a great idea! However, there can be some pitfalls along the way, so before you pick up your hammer and nails, make sure you do your homework.

ZONING

If your neighborhood is not zoned for a secondary suite, and you add one anyway, be prepared for a visit from an inspector from your city or municipality. If your tenant is noisy, or your neighbors just don't like the idea of living next door to a rental suite, one call to city hall and your little income booster is history.

Many municipalities have a kind of "don't ask, don't tell" philosophy on secondary suites. In the city I live in, many homes have such units and they are legal—"legal" in the sense that they meet legal standards required for a secondary suite, such as a separate entrance, windows as an alternate means of emergency escape and smoke alarms. They may meet the legal building standards, but as far as the city is concerned, they are unauthorized. You can, according to the law, have a family member or nanny live in the suite, and basically that's it. So, although the city knows that a suite has probably been rented to tenants, (heck, they charge extra for garbage pick-up for suite-ed homes), it will do nothing to enforce the law. Whether it's because they are too difficult to police or too tricky to legislate, secondary suites have my city hall looking the other way. Consequently, many of these suites are rented out— but there is always the chance that if a tenant creates a problem for whatever reason, such that the neighbours become annoyed, that suite could be shut down. (Truthfully, though, it's not likely to happen: many of the neighbours have tenanted suites, too. You don't want to bite the hand that feeds.) In fact, the real estate board will not let you refer to these suites as "mortgage helpers." You can call them "in-law" or "nanny" suites, and that's pretty much it. Any mention of deriving an income from them is strictly *verboten.*

The majority of homes in my area that have secondary suites were built with them in place, not added to a home afterward. Adding a suite to an existing home would require some extra work. You may need to upgrade your wiring and electrical panel, add plumbing and perhaps a separate entrance. You certainly don't want to add to your home without checking to make sure your changes don't inadvertently create a fire hazard, or worse.

ADDING A SUITE

If you have checked with your municipality and there is no bylaw preventing it, you may want to pursue adding a secondary suite. If you're purchasing a home that doesn't have one, and you have checked the zoning and decide that adding a suite makes sense, make sure you get an experienced and reliable contractor in to provide an estimate. For instance, if the electrical panel requires upgrading and all new plumbing and wiring needs to be installed, and that's just for starters—you may end up with some prohibitive costs. Before you remove subjects on the purchase of any home that you plan to add a suite, make sure that option is viable.

You'll also need to ask yourself several questions: Will there be a separate laundry facility for the tenant, or will they share a main laundry? What will be the entrance to the secondary suite? What kind of parking will be available for the tenant? All these questions will factor into whether adding a suite is a wise decision. If the home you're considering is small to start with, maybe using the entire basement for a suite might make your own living arrangements a little cramped.

But there's more to it than just calculating what adding a suite will cost. You have to be realistic about what the suite will actually *add* to your bottom line. Many people like the idea of having a "mortgage" helper, but they don't do the research to find out exactly how much that suite is going to bolster the bottom line.

First of all, how is the local rental market? Chances are, if you own a home with a suite in it, and you live close to a university or college, you'll have no shortage of tenants. Things like good transportation links will be very important. However, certain conditions can lead to a more competitive rental market, and that could cost you. For instance, if you have a suite that you are relying on as an income producer, and the real estate market is heavily favoring buyers, you may find yourself having to reduce what you're asking in monthly rent. That's partly because people who might have tried selling have decided not to sell after all, and rent their home out instead. That may create more competition, and thus lower rent, for you.

If you're planning to add a suite or upgrade an existing one, make sure you don't go overboard. Remember, this

isn't for you to live in—it's something that you aspire
to keep low-maintenance, but you want to present in an
inviting way without spending a small fortune. You must
know your target audience and what kind of rent your suite
can generate. It doesn't make sense to install professional-
grade appliances and hand-stripped hardwood floors
in a suite that will rent for no more than $800 a month.
Be reasonable. Good-quality laminate flooring is easy
to maintain and will wear much better than carpeting.
Higher-end appliances can often be found at second-hand
stores or on websites such as Craigslist. Little touches that
don't cost a lot, such as baseboards and crown mouldings,
can give the suite an upscale look that may generate a
higher rent and attract good tenants. Adding inexpensive
closet organizers and other cheap and cheery touches can
do wonders. So does a nice neutral paint. Don't forget
good-quality lighting, particularly if there is not a lot of
natural light in the suite. It's the little things that will often
add value to a mortgage helper and make a good tenant
want to stay. This will help your bottom line.

TAX IMPLICATIONS

I'm no accountant (if you want proof of that, just ask *my*
accountant), but it stands to reason that you will have to
pay tax on income derived from a tenancy. Take this into
account when you consider a secondary suite, as it could

affect your bottom line. If you don't declare this income, you do so at your own risk. Canada Revenue Agency is not known for big hugs and tax forgiveness, and you will pay back interest and a lot more if you get caught.

TENANTS

The rules of tenancy are different from province to province, but if you're planning to be a landlord, I will tell you right now: the law favours the tenant. DO YOUR HOMEWORK. Here are some of the top issues you might run into.

Leases

You may think that a lease will protect you as a landlord, but that may not be the case. The laws surrounding leases vary in each province. For instance, in BC, a lease must specify an ending date with vacant possession. If no date is specified on the lease, then at the end of the term it will become a month to month tenancy. *So, in BC, unless the end date and vacancy are specified in the lease, the tenant does not have to vacate at the end of the term.* Landlords can terminate that tenancy only for specified reasons set out in legislation. In other provinces, different regulations apply. Make sure you've checked the most recent legislation for your province or territory—most of which can be found online.

Generally speaking, though, a fixed-term lease is often your best route for tenancy. It can always be renegotiated, but to have a fixed-term and a move-out date will help protect a landlord. Again, every province varies, but it is much more difficult to evict a month-to-month tenant. Legislation tends to take the side of the renter, and it can be very costly to evict, especially if the tenant puts up a fight. It's not just the legal fees or your time, but also the possibility that your tenant may not be paying their rent.

Pets

Again, the rules differ between provinces. In BC and Alberta, you can restrict or prohibit pets, but Ontario legislation precludes that. Nova Scotia allows landlords to change rules regarding pets, but it must be within a certain time frame before the expiry of a lease. If you're a private home owner, you have latitude that may not be available in an apartment complex, but that doesn't allow you to violate legislation. It should be noted, though, that many of my clients who have rental suites prefer to have tenants with pets. Since in BC pets can be restricted by the landlord, a rental that allows them is often difficult to find, and a good tenant will appreciate that. Try to be open minded: you may think you don't want a tenant with a large dog, but that dog might sleep all day!

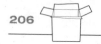

Smoking

Check to make sure whether you can legally restrict the tenant. Most people will smoke outside their homes if they do smoke, but if you're the landlord living upstairs, that may bother you. Make sure this issue is addressed, and if it's very important to you, specify it in the lease.

Children

It is generally illegal to refuse to rent to people with children. (Exceptions apply: obviously, a retirement complex would not rent to people with children, and that would be stated in their bylaws.) However, the grounds for refusal are often difficult to support. If a person begins renting as a single person, and then has a child while still a tenant, that would not be grounds for eviction.

Utilities

Make sure the tenancy agreement clearly states who is to pay for utilities. Some landlords will bill a tenant a portion of the monthly bill for heat and hot water, and for cable as well. Others will analyse their annual bills and take into account the extra costs and factor it into the actual rent (for example, specifying that rent includes heat and hot water). Make sure you have thought of these costs and factored them in appropriately.

Don't Forget:

- Check your local legislation regarding bylaw zoning for rental suites.

- ALWAYS CHECK A PROSPECTIVE TENANT'S REFERENCES! Anybody can put on clean clothes and act the part. This means you must do a credit check, talk to current and previous landlords and confirm employment status. Don't think you can be a good judge of character. The prospective tenant may be the nicest person in the world, but may be the nicest person who can't afford to pay the rent most months.

- Have a contingency plan. If you cannot afford to live in the home without having the suite tenanted full time, you may want to reconsider purchasing the home altogether. Maintenance, tenant turnover and possible damage costs that you can't recover may turn that great idea of the nifty basement mortgage helper into a nightmare. You will need to have a financial cushion to help you through any interruption of the rental income.

- Make sure you research the rental market in your area. To miss this vital step could cost you big time in the long run. You might invest too much in your rental suite, and not be able to generate the rent that would make those expenditures viable. Or worse, you may rent for much less than the unit is worth, and thus be limited as to how much you could increase the rent annually, based on the residential tenancy act that applies to you.

KEEP IT SIMPLE?

As you can probably tell, there are a lot of things to consider when having a secondary suite in your home. In many ways, it can be a job in itself! Many home owners will rely on a professional rental agent to manage these issues. The agent will find and screen tenants, collect rent, and if there's a problem, deal with it directly. Of course, these services will cost you, but it might be worth the peace of mind. A licensed rentals agent knows the laws that apply in your province or territory, and will be up to date with any changes you may not be aware of. If you want all the financial benefits of having a tenant but none of the hassle, this might be your best option.

A FINAL WORD

We've reached the end of the book, but I hope it's the beginning of a wonderful adventure in home buying—or selling—for you. It's my hope that you feel confident about buying or selling your home, regardless if this is the first time out the gate or you've gone down this path several times before. Like I said at the outset, you don't need to be bogged down with all sorts of fancy terminology, but you do need a bit of awareness when you decide to make a move—and it should be an exciting time, not a frightening one!

Home ownership will most likely be the biggest investment you will make in your life, so don't be afraid to ask questions. Never do anything that makes you uncomfortable, and don't sign anything that you haven't read first! Simple advice, really, but often buyers and sellers for some reason feel "embarrassed" about asking questions, because they are afraid of looking foolish for not knowing the answers! In reality, the only thing worse than not asking questions, is NOT KNOWING WHICH QUESTIONS TO ASK. Hopefully, this book has helped!

Good luck, and all the best in your future real estate adventure!

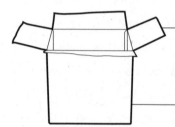

GLOSSARY OF TERMS YOU MAY ENCOUNTER ALONG THE WAY!

Acceleration clause: A clause written into a mortgage agreement to allow the lender to accelerate or call the entire principal balance of the mortgage, plus accrued interest, when the borrower is delinquent with payments.

Adjusted cost base (ACB): The value of real property established for tax purposes. It is the original cost plus any allowable capital improvements, certain acquisition costs and any mortgage interest costs, less any depreciation.

Agreement of purchase and sale: A written agreement between the owner and a purchaser for the purchase of real estate for a predetermined price and terms.

Amenities: Generally, those parts of the condominium or apartment building that are intended to beautify the premises and that are for the enjoyment of occupants rather than for utility.

Amortization period: The actual number of years it will take to repay a mortgage loan in full. This can be well in excess of the loan's term. For example, mortgages often have five-year terms but 25-year amortization periods.

Amortization: The reduction of a loan through periodic payments in which interest is charged only on the unpaid balance.

Analysis of property: The systematic method of determining the performance of investment real estate using a property analysis form.

Appraised value: An estimate of the fair-market value of the property, usually performed by an appraiser.

Arrears: Arrears are the overdue payments owing on either a mortgage or a lease; it also refers to the state of being late in fulfilling the obligations of the mortgage or lease agreement.

Assessment fee: A monthly fee that condominium owners must pay, usually including management fees, costs of common property upkeep, heating costs, garbage-removal costs, the owner's contribution to the contingency reserve fund, and so on. In the case of time-shares, the fee is normally levied annually. Also referred to as the maintenance fee.

Assign: The act of transferring ownership of or responsibility for a property to a purchaser or tenant; usually a step that occurs prior to the original owner or tenant completing the purchase or lease term. The assignee assumes the right to purchase a property, or becomes the subtenant of the original tenant.

Assumption agreement: A legal document signed by a home buyer that requires the buyer to assume responsibility for the obligations of a mortgage made by a former owner.

Balance sheet: A financial statement that indicates the financial status of a condominium corporation or apartment building, or other revenue property, at a specific point in time by listing its assets and liabilities.

Blended payments: Equal payments consisting of both a principal and an interest component, paid each month during the term of the mortgage. The principal portion increases each month, while the interest portion decreases, but the total monthly payment does not change.

Budget: An annual estimate of a condominium corporation or apartment building's expenses and the revenues needed to balance those expenses. There are operating budgets and capital budgets. (See also *Capital budget.*)

Canada Mortgage and Housing Corporation (CMHC): The federal Crown corporation that administers the National Housing Act. CMHC services include providing housing information and assistance, financing, and insuring home-purchase loans for lenders.

Canadian Real Estate Association (CREA): An association of members of the real estate industry, principally real estate agents and brokers.

Capital budget: An estimate of costs to cover replacements and improvements, and the corresponding revenues needed to balance them, usually for a 12-month period. Different from an operating budget.

Capital gain: Profit on the sale of an asset that is subject to taxation.

Capital improvements. Major improvements made to a property that are written off over several years rather than expensed off in the year in which they are made.

Charge: A document registered against a property, stating that someone has or believes he or she has a claim on the property.

Closing costs: The expenses over and above the purchase price of buying and selling real estate.

Closing date: The date on which the sale of a property becomes final and the new owner takes possession.

Closing: The actual completion of the transaction acknowledging satisfaction of all legal and financial obligations between buyer and seller, and acknowledging the deed or transfer of title and disbursement of funds to appropriate parties.

Collateral mortgage: A loan backed up by a promissory note and the security of a mortgage on a property. The money borrowed may be used for the purchase of a property or for another purpose, such as home renovations or a vacation.

Common area maintenance fee: The charge to owners to maintain the common areas, normally due on a monthly basis.

Common area: The area in a condominium project that is shared by all of the condominium owners, such as elevators, hallways, and parking lots.

Condominium corporation: The condominium association of unit owners incorporated under some provincial condominium legislation, automatically at the time of registration of the project. It is called a strata corporation in British Columbia. Under each of the provincial statutes, it will differ from an ordinary corporation in many respects. The condominium corporation, unlike a private business corporation, usually does not enjoy limited liability, and any judgement against the corporation for the payment of money is usually a judgement against each owner. The objects of the corporation are to manage the property and any assets of the corporation, and its duties include effecting compliance by the owners with the requirements of the Act, the declaration, the bylaws, and the rules.

Condominium council: The governing body of the condominium corporation, elected at the annual general meeting of the corporation.

Condominium: A housing unit to which the owner has title and of which the owner also owns a share in the common area (such as elevators, hallways, swimming pool and land).

Conventional mortgage: A mortgage loan that does not exceed 75 percent of the appraised value or of the purchase price of the property, whichever is the less. Mortgages that exceed this limit generally must be insured by mortgage insurance, such as that provided by CMHC and GEM.

Conversion: The changing of a structure from some other use, such as a rental apartment to a condominium apartment.

Conveyancing: The transfer of property, or title to property, from one party to another.

Credit bureau: An agency that maintains credit files, such as Equifax and others.

Credit check: A report typically run to review the credit history of an individual to assist in determining whether or not the individual is worthy of receiving credit.

Credit rating: The score—usually expressed as a number —calculated using information in an individual's credit file. The credit rating is typically used to determine credit worthiness. The better the score, the more worthy of credit an individual is.

Debt service: Cost of paying interest for use of mortgage money.

Deed: This document conveys the title of the property to the purchaser. Different terminology may be used in different provincial jurisdictions.

Depreciation: The amount by which a property owner writes off the value of a real estate investment over the life of the investment. Depreciation is not applicable to the value of land.

Down payment: An initial amount of money (in the form of cash) put forward by the purchaser. Usually it represents the difference between the purchase price and the amount of the mortgage loan.

Equity return: The percentage ratio between an owner's equity in a property and the total of cash flow plus mortgage principal reduction.

Equity: The difference between the price for which a property could be sold and the total debts registered against it.

Escrow: The holding of a deed or contract by a third party until fulfillment of certain stipulated conditions between the contracting parties.

Estate: The title or interest one has in property such as real estate and personal property that can, if desired, be passed on to survivors at the time of one's death.

Fair-market value: The value established on real property that is determined to be one that a buyer is willing to pay and for which a seller is willing to sell.

Fee simple: A manner of owning land, in one's own name and free of any conditions, limitations, or restrictions.

Financial statements: Documents that show the financial status of the condominium corporation, apartment building, or other revenue property at a given point in time. Generally includes income and expense statement and balance sheet.

Floating-rate mortgage: Another term for variable-rate mortgage.

Foreclosure: A legal procedure whereby the lender obtains ownership of, or the right to sell, the property following default by the borrower.

Freehold: The outright ownership of land, or land and buildings; differs from **leasehold**.

GE Mortgage Insurance Canada (GEM): A private company providing mortgage insurance in Canada.

GEM: The initials for GE Mortgage Insurance Canada. See **GE Mortgage Insurance Canada**.

Guarantor: A party that guarantees to pay the debts of an individual in the event the individual is unable to pay the debts.

Guarantor's letter: A legal document by which the guarantor agrees to assume the debt of another party.

High-ratio mortgage: A conventional mortgage loan that exceeds 75 percent of the appraised value or purchase price of the property. Such a mortgage must be insured.

Highrise: Any multi-unit residential building of six or more storeys.

Income, gross: Income or cash flow before expenses.

Income, net: Income or cash flow after expenses (but generally before income tax).

Interest averaging: The method of determining the overall average interest rate being paid when more than one mortgage is involved.

Interim financing: The temporary financing by a lender during the construction of real property for resale, or while awaiting other funds.

Judgement: The official outcome of a lawsuit or other legal proceeding. The judgement may be financial or otherwise.

Legal description: Identification of a property that is recognized by law, that identifies that property from all others.

Lessee: The tenant in rental space.

Lessor: The owner of the rental space.

Letter of intent: Used in place of a formal written contract with a deposit. The prospective purchaser informs the seller, in writing, that he or she is willing to enter into a formal purchase contract upon certain terms and conditions if they are acceptable to the seller.

Leverage: The use of financing or other people's money to control large pieces of real property with a small amount of invested capital.

Limited partnership: An investment group in which one partner serves as the general partner and the others as limited partners. The general partner bears all of the financial responsibility and management of the investment. The limited partners are obligated only to the extent of their original investment plus possible personal guarantees.

Listings, exclusive agency: A signed agreement by a seller in which he or she agrees to co-operate with one broker. All other brokers must go through the listing broker.

Listings, multiple: (See also *Multiple Listing Service*.) A system of agency/sub-agency relationships. If Broker A lists the property for sale, "A" is the vendor's agent. If Broker B sees the MLS listing and offers it for sale, "B" is the vendor's sub-agent.

Listings, open: A listing given to one or more brokers, none of whom have any exclusive rights or control over the sale, by other brokers or the owner of the property.

Marginal tax rate: That point in income at which any additional income will be taxed at a higher tax rate.

MLS: See *Multiple Listing Service.*

Mortgage wraparound: Sometimes called an all-inclusive mortgage. A mortgage that includes any existing mortgages on the property. The buyer makes one large payment on the wraparound and the seller continues making the existing mortgage payments out of that payment.

Mortgage, balloon: A mortgage amortized over a number of years, but that requires the entire principal balance to be paid at a certain time, short of the full amortization period.

Mortgage, constant: The interest rate charged on a mortgage consisting of both the rate being charged by the lender and the rate that represents the amount of principal reduction each period.

Mortgage, deferred payment: A mortgage allowing for payments to be made on a deferred or delayed basis. Usually used where present income is not sufficient to make the payments.

Mortgage, discounted: The selling of a mortgage to another party at a discount or an amount less than the face value of the mortgage.

Mortgage, first: A mortgage placed on a property in first position.

Mortgage, fixed: This is a conventional mortgage, with payments of interest and principal. Fixed terms with a fixed rate can vary from six months to 10 years or more.

Mortgage, insurance: Insurance provided by the lender as an option for the borrower. It would pay out the balance outstanding on the mortgage, in the event of the borrower's death.

Mortgage, interest only: Payments are made only of interest; the payment does not reduce the principal of the debt.

Mortgage, points: The interest rate charged by the lender.

Mortgage, second: A mortgage placed on a property in second position to an already existing first mortgage.

Mortgage, variable: A mortgage with an interest rate that fluctuates with the Bank of Canada interest rate. The mortgagee just pays the interest, with optional pay-down on the principal. Different from a fixed-rate mortgage (see *Mortgage, fixed*).

Mortgage: The document that pledges real property as collateral for an indebtedness.

Mortgagee: The lender.

Mortgagor: The borrower.

Multiple Listing Service (MLS): A service licensed to member real estate boards by the Canadian Real Estate Association. Used to compile and disseminate information by publication and computer concerning a given property to a large number of agents and brokers.

National Housing Act (NHA) Loan: A mortgage loan that is insured by Canada Mortgage and Housing Corp. to certain maximums.

Offer to purchase: The document that sets forth all the terms and conditions under which a purchaser offers to purchase property. This offer, when accepted by the seller, becomes a binding agreement of purchase and sale once all conditions have been removed.

Operating budget: An estimate of costs to operate a building or condominium complex and corresponding revenues needed to balance them, usually for a 12- month period. Different from a capital budget.

Operating costs: Those expenses required to operate an investment property, generally excluding mortgage payments.

Option agreement: A contract, with consideration, given to a purchaser of a property, giving him or her the right to purchase at a future date. If the individual chooses not to purchase, the deposit is forfeited to the seller.

Personal property: Property in an investment property, such as carpeting, draperies and refrigerators, that can be depreciated over a shorter useful life than the structure itself.

PI: Principal and interest due on a mortgage.

PIT: Principal, interest, and taxes due on a mortgage.

Prepayment penalty: A penalty charge written into many mortgages that must be paid if the mortgage is paid off ahead of schedule.

Principal: The amount the purchaser actually borrowed, or the portion of it still owing on the original loan.

Property manager: A manager or management company hired to run an investment property for the owner.

Purchase-and-sale agreement: See *Agreement of purchase and sale*.

Tax shelter: The tax write-off possible through the depreciation benefits available on investment real estate ownership.

Title insurance: This insurance covers the purchaser or vendor in case of any defects in the property or title, that existed at the time of sale but which were not known until after completion of the sale.

Title: Generally, the evidence of right that a person has to the possession of property.

Trust account: The separate account in which a lawyer or real estate broker holds funds until the real estate closing takes place or other legal disbursement is made.

Trust funds: Funds held in trust, either as a deposit for the purchase of real property or to pay taxes and insurance.

Unit: Normally refers to the rental suite or that part of a condominium owned and occupied or rented by the owner.

Useful life: The term during which an asset is expected to have useful value.

Utilities: Any one of the array of services that allow a property to function, and which typically deliver a basic social good, such as heat, water and electricity, or phone and television service. The landlord may provide access to utilities for a fee, or the tenant may be responsible for arranging a connection to the utilities.

Value, assessed: The property value as determined by local, regional, or provincial assessment authority.

Vendor take-back: A procedure wherein the seller (vendor) of a property provides some or all of the mortgage financing in order to sell the property. Also referred to as vendor financing.

Vendor: A person selling a piece of property.

Zoning: Rules for land use established by local governments.

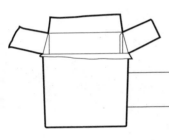

INDEX